simple prayers POWERFUL RESULTS

A Six-Week Bible Study
on Discovering God's
Wisdom and Will

JANE GLENCHUR

warnerpress

Warner Press, Inc.
Warner Press and Warner Press logo are trademarks of Warner Press, Inc.
Simple Prayers, Powerful Results: A Six-Week Bible Study on Discovering God's Wisdom and Will
Written by Jane Glenchur

Requests for information should be sent to:
Warner Press, Inc.
2902 Enterprise Drive
Anderson, IN 46013
www.warnerpress.org

Editors: Julie Campbell, Robin Loisch
Cover and Layout by Curtis Corzine

ISBN: 9781684345205
Printed in USA

DEDICATION

To Amelia and Mark: You are the living answers to my many prayers for a family. You make my heart sing. You are the reason I have diligently sought the Lord on how to pray and how to have a personal relationship with Him.

Table of Contents

Introduction

Week 1

Week 2

Week 3

Week 4

Week 5

Week 6

INTRODUCTION

I was the first to drop down into the deep, dark opening of the cave while the rest of the class waited above. The silence and impenetrable blackness threatened to overwhelm me, but I knew I was not alone. Prayer can be like that, at times. We find a private place and seclude ourselves to be with God. We speak our fears out loud to Him in our dark times. We're hungry for a response, but many times it seems like we only hear the echo of our own voice bouncing off the cave walls. We do all the talking and none of the listening.

The Lord is reaching out to each one of us. *Call to me and I will answer you* (Jeremiah 33:3, NIV). He longs to speak with you and me. Yet many times we have not learned how to tune in to His voice. Perhaps you are wondering: What is God's will for my life? For my family? How will I know if He's speaking to me? Questions like those used to hound me. I had to know!

Calling to God, or prayer, is my passion, but it wasn't always this way. Prayer was not something I learned growing up. The only prayers in our home were at meals when we said grace.

I had no concept of a loving heavenly Father who longed to interact with me daily through prayer. God seemed light-years away, too busy with running the planet to even notice me, let alone want a relationship with me. My concept of Him was probably related to the lack of a close relationship with my earthly father, who left our family in my teen years. Maybe some of you can relate to my experience.

After years of wandering away from what little faith I had, I committed my life to Christ right before entering medical school. The next frenzied nine years of school and residency left no time for me to study the Bible. Most of my prayers were desperate "Help me, God" pleas. Perhaps you've prayed a few of those too.

It took a malpractice lawsuit to start me on the road to a life of intimacy with the Lord and amazing, personal answers to prayer. Little did I know what He had in store for me as He took my life and turned it right side up!

I love reading God's Word. The Scriptures are loaded with spiritual wisdom, but I also wanted practical answers to everyday problems that aren't found in Scripture. Jeremiah 33:3 (NIV) was my answer. Here is the verse in its entirety:

> *Call to me and I will answer you and tell you* ***great and unsearchable things you do not know*** (emphasis added).

I decided to take God's promise and apply it to my life. He invites you and me to call to Him. God promises to answer, and He promises to reveal hidden things that we know nothing about…yet.

God is calling to each one of us, but so often we are too busy, too distracted, or just not convinced that He really cares about all the details and problems in our lives. That's how I felt until I got sued. Sheer terror and desperation drove me to my knees, seeking answers to problems I could not solve on my own.

God is looking for us, His children, to partner with Him in all of life. If it matters to you, it matters to Him, whether the issue is big or small. If you need comfort, solutions to problems, or financial breakthrough, you can learn to tap into God's unlimited wisdom and access His blessings.

Are you curious about those hidden things that God wants you to discover by connecting with Him in prayer? I am excited to share with you what I have learned about prayer. Please join me over the next six weeks as we explore the heart of God for us and His desire that we call on Him. Let's get started!

God is looking for us,

HIS CHILDREN,

to partner with Him
in all of life.

**IF IT MATTERS TO YOU,
IT MATTERS TO HIM,**

whether the issue is

BIG OR SMALL.

WEEK 1

DAY 1: The Importance of Prayer

Devastated! I had prayed the same prayer for seven years: "Lord, please don't let me get sued!"

How could God have allowed this to happen? A malpractice lawsuit—every physician's worst nightmare—yet here in my hand lay a thick sheaf of papers telling me that a patient was suing me for a supposed misdiagnosis.

Would we lose our house? All our savings? My job?

Perhaps you, too, have wondered why God didn't answer a prayer the way you wanted. Maybe you've questioned whether He even cares about your concerns. Does He even know you exist?

Anger, hurt, and fear took up residence in my mind and emotions for months. Little did I know that the very thing the enemy planned to use to destroy me would be the very thing that God would use for His glory and my spiritual growth. That malpractice suit was the Lord's ticket to usher me into the gift and mystery of prayer. But it didn't happen overnight.

Please join me as we travel up and down the valleys and mountaintops of prayer, as we learn the importance and blessings a rich prayer life can bring. Whether you are in a spiritual desert or an oasis, or somewhere in between, God has hidden treasures that are waiting to be uncovered.

Let's start with a brief survey to get a baseline on your prayer life.

1. Have you ever been disappointed by an unanswered prayer? Record your thoughts.

____

____

____

2. What was your reaction? You can check one or more.

❑ Anger ❑ Hurt ❑ Discouragement ❑ Fear ❑ Other

Describe: ____________________________________

____

____

3. As a result, did you…?

- ❑ Give up on God and stop praying ❑ Pray harder
- ❑ Seek wise counsel ❑ Continue to trust God despite not understanding why
- ❑ Other

Explain: ______________________________

____

____

4. Is prayer your first recourse when you need comfort or wisdom? Or is it your last resort? Explain:

____

____

____

5. Do you have a regular time set aside to pray, or is it hit or miss whenever you can squeeze it in?

____

____

____

Perhaps you wonder: Is prayer necessary when God is all powerful (omnipotent), all knowing (omniscient), and all present (omnipresent)? To answer that question, we need to go back in Scripture to the beginning of creation. What does Genesis 1:26 tell us?

____

____

____

God made mankind in His image and gave us authority over His creation. As a result, we see that God limited Himself to co-labor with us, His family. We are stewards over the entire earth. That's a heavy responsibility, isn't it? Do you think we might need His help to succeed in that task? I know I do!

We read in Genesis 3:8–19 that there was dialogue between God and Adam and

Eve. They spoke to each other, and that is the essence of prayer. Prayer is talking and listening to God.

Unfortunately, because of Adam's sin, all mankind is born with a fallen nature, a propensity to disobey God. We see that throughout the history of God's chosen people, the Israelites. When their sin reached a certain level, God would bring judgment upon them to turn them away from their rebellious behavior and to draw them back into right relationship with Him. What does God say to the prophet in Ezekiel 22:30?

____

____

____

Verses 17– 29 tell us why God was looking for someone to repent on behalf of the sins of the Israelites. What sins were they committing that angered God?

____

____

____

What does 2 Peter 3:9 tell us about God's character?

____

____

____

The Lord is merciful and longs to forgive. God loves His children and wants to spare us judgment, but because He is holy, He must judge sin. God wants to co-labor with mankind and searches for someone who will pray and repent on behalf of the people—a mediator or advocate.

Let's look at two examples from the Old Testament of what it means to stand in the gap. Moses stood in the gap for the Israelites shortly after their exodus from slavery in Egypt. While Moses was meeting with the Lord on Mt. Sinai to receive the Ten Commandments, the people grew weary of waiting and came to Aaron demanding that he make a god for them to worship. Aaron fashioned a calf made from the gold earrings that the people gave him. When the Lord saw them worshiping the golden calf, His anger burned against the people. What does the Lord tell Moses in

Exodus 32:9?

What is Moses' response in verses 11–13?

Is Moses effective in his plea on behalf of the Israelites? (See verse 14).

Moses stood in the gap, and the Israelites were spared. The Lord listened to his prayer and relented from His anger.

The prophet Elijah is our second example. He lived during the reign of King Ahab. According to 1 Kings 16:30 (NIV), King Ahab *did more evil in the eyes of the LORD than any of those before him.* Instead of worshiping God, he set up altars to the false gods, Baal and Asherah. What judgment resulted from Ahab's idolatry? See 1 Kings 17:1.

Please read 1 Kings 18 to understand the significance of Elijah's mediation between the people and God. After three years of drought, the Lord instructs Elijah to meet with Ahab, and He will then send rain.

Elijah goes to the king with a challenge. Ahab is to bring all the false prophets of Baal and Asherah and all the people to Mt. Carmel for a showdown. Briefly describe the faceoff between Elijah and the prophets of Baal below.

In 1 Kings 18:27–38, what results do the false prophets get compared with what happens when Elijah calls on the name of his God?

In verse 39 the people respond by saying, *The Lord—he is God!* Everything went up in smoke, including their false beliefs. Elijah then climbs to the top of the mountain to intercede a second time. This time to end the drought. A heavy downpour ensues.

These two examples clearly indicate that God will listen to just one person who prays on behalf of an entire nation. That's the power of prayer!

We will see in the weeks to come how important *your* prayers are. You don't have to be a prophet or have a special calling on your life to call on God. Look what He promises you in Jeremiah 29:13 (NIV): *You will seek me and find me when you seek me with all your heart.* Your prayers may make the difference between blessing and want. They may be the turning point in your life or your loved ones' lives.

Let's look at a bit more of Old Testament history so we can then appreciate how unique our relationship to God is now, under the new covenant we have through Jesus Christ.

God gave Moses very detailed instructions on Mt. Sinai for building the tabernacle or "tent of meeting"—the place where God would meet with those who would be set apart and consecrated as priests. The priests became the official mediators to stand in the gap for the Israelites as they wandered through the desert wilderness for forty years, heading to the Promised Land. The tabernacle was the forerunner of the Jewish temple that Solomon would later build in Jerusalem.

Read Exodus 40:12–15. What four things did the Lord command Moses to do regarding Aaron and his sons in their roles as priests, or mediators?

Since God is holy, only those who were appointed by Him and who were cleansed, anointed, and consecrated were allowed to come into the tabernacle. Ordinary people were forbidden.

Read Numbers 18:7. What would happen to anyone who was not consecrated as a priest, but who tried to enter the tabernacle?

____

____

____

Under the old covenant, God would only allow a priest to offer the blood sacrifices necessary to atone for their own sins and those of the people. The priests could enter the Holy Place where the altar of incense was located. The fragrance of burning incense symbolized their prayers being offered up to God.

A curtain or veil separated the Holy Place from the Holy of Holies where the ark of the covenant was kept. Only the high priest was allowed to enter the Holy of Holies one day a year, on Yom Kippur, to meet with God and atone for the sins of the Israelites.

We have seen individual mediators like Moses and Elijah plead with God for mercy on behalf of the Israelites. Then we read about the establishment of the Old Testament priesthood in order to atone for the sins of God's chosen people. Tomorrow we will look at the differences between the old and new covenants and learn who the new covenant advocates are.

Returning to my lawsuit: Where was God in all this? He hadn't answered my prayers the way I had hoped. I was warned not to talk to a soul about the lawsuit, not even my family. I wasn't even allowed to journal my thoughts. I had nowhere else to turn… except to God!

What I had learned years before in a semester at law school haunted me as well. I knew that the legal system often handed down unfair judgments against innocent people. Would it find me liable too?

The thought of being grilled on a witness stand terrified me. Wasn't there some way out? Not according to my attorney. During a visit to his office, he looked at me sternly and warned, "Get it in your head. This *is* going to trial."

"Well, I believe in miracles. I don't think it has to go to trial," I replied with a mustard seed of faith.

Ten months later the lawsuit was dropped! Victory! I got my miracle.

During those ten months of preparing for trial mentally, emotionally, and spiritually, God began to teach me the power and importance of prayer. Over the next six weeks, I will be sharing with you those pearls of wisdom forged in my refiner's fire.

As we progress through this study, I hope you will see the importance of making prayer a priority, if it is not already. You will be acquiring tools to help you develop a consistent prayer life that is meaningful and rewarding. There is no magic formula, but we will talk about various ways to pray and pitfalls to avoid. Please continue along with me on the journey of discovering how to partner with God and experience your own amazing answers to prayer.

DAY 2: The Old and New Covenants

As an extremely shy child, many times when someone asked my name, I would look to my older brother imploringly. He would respond, "Her name is Jane." Big brother was my mediator, in a sense. He spoke for me. As I prepared for my malpractice trial, my attorney mediated between me and my accuser.

In yesterday's lesson we saw examples of mediators—those who take the place of another or represent one to another. In the accounts of Moses and Elijah, we learned that even *one* person can pray on behalf of many, even a nation, and God hears and responds to those prayers.

The Old Testament gives us a history of God's special relationship to Israel. He established the law to make them aware of sin, and the sacrificial system to temporarily cleanse them of sin. Unfortunately, the Israelites repeatedly failed to keep God's law and fell under His judgment many times.

However, the prophet Jeremiah foretells that something better is coming. Read Jeremiah 31:31–34. What does God promise the Israelites?

____

____

____

The law was a shadow of a better covenant to come as prophesied by Jeremiah. In the new covenant, God promised to wipe away every sin forever. That's good news!

Read Hebrews 9:11–15. Who is the mediator of this new covenant and why?

____

____

____

Jesus Christ is the mediator of the new covenant. In the New Testament, or new covenant, we see Jesus symbolically in the role of high priest. Instead of making animal sacrifices to pay for sins, Jesus willingly submitted to crucifixion, shedding His own blood as a sinless, perfect Lamb of God, in order to pay for the sins of all who would accept Him as their Lord and Savior. How does 1 Timothy 2:5 describe Jesus?

____

____

____

Why is Jesus especially suited to be our mediator with God? See Hebrews 4:15.

It is comforting to know that Jesus walked this earth in human flesh, endured temptations, and therefore can sympathize with our human weaknesses. He was fully God and fully human, and He knows our struggles.

Read Hebrews 7:23–28. How long did the earthly priests serve?

How long does Jesus serve as our mediator, and how often does He intercede or pray for us?

I find this very reassuring. Jesus stands in the gap for us with the Father. We serve a holy God whose sinless Son prays for us *every* day.

Let's look at a few differences between the old covenant and the new covenant. The old covenant was only for the Israelites (Deuteronomy 4:7–8) and came by way of Moses, while the new covenant came through Jesus and includes anyone who believes in Him as their Savior. The old covenant exposes sin. The new covenant wipes away sin. Many high priests served for their lifetime, but we only have one High Priest who serves for eternity.

Describe in your own words how the new covenant compares to the old as mentioned in Hebrews 8:6.

Read Hebrews 9:23–28. Describe how Christ's sacrifice differed from the animal sacrifices the priests would make to atone for sin.

Where there is forgiveness of sin, there is no longer any need to offer a sacrifice for sin. Under the old covenant, the blood of animals covered over sins, but under the new covenant, Christ's blood removed sin. Otherwise, Jesus would have to offer Himself again and again.

What is the assurance God gives us in Hebrews 10:17–18? Write the verses below:

What does Jesus' atonement and role as mediator enable us to do? See Hebrews 4:16.

This passage assures us that we are worthy to make our petitions before God's throne of grace, not because of good works, but because of God's mercy and grace. We are saved by grace, not works, so that we cannot boast in ourselves or in our good deeds (see Ephesians 2:8–9). We come into God's presence not because of what we have done, but because of what Christ has done for us.

Something quite astonishing happened in the temple right at the moment of Christ's crucifixion. What does Matthew tell us in chapter 27, verses 50–51?

The curtain that separated the Holy Place from the Holy of Holies (where only the high priest could enter) tore from top to bottom, symbolizing that there was no longer a barrier between God and people. As believers in Christ, we can approach

God through our prayers at any time! His throne room is always open. God is never too busy to hear our prayers. So go boldly whenever your need arises!

Read 1 Peter 2:4–5, 9. How does Peter describe believers?

____

____

____

Not only do we have a high priest in Jesus Christ, but the apostle Peter describes us as a royal priesthood and our bodies as a spiritual house for Christ to indwell. We now offer spiritual sacrifices rather than blood sacrifices. But what are spiritual sacrifices?

Romans 12:1–2 describes those sacrifices. Describe them in your own words below:

____

____

____

To be living sacrifices means to devote ourselves to serving the Lord, allowing Him to sanctify us. Sanctification is a lifelong process in which God is changing our hearts and making us more like Him.

For more clarity on being a living sacrifice, read James 1:21–22. Rewrite it in your own words.

____

____

____

By renewing our minds with the Word of God, Romans 12:2 assures us that we will know what the will of God is for our lives. How often have I asked the Lord, "What do You want me to do in this situation?" I'm sure you probably have too. Knowing Scripture informs us about how to live in a manner pleasing to the Lord and teaches us how to pray for ourselves and others. His Word is His will.

But perhaps you are wondering, why pray since God already knows your need? Let's see what Jesus says in Matthew 7:7–11. What three things does He exhort us to do?

____

____

____

I find it interesting that the first letters of ask, seek, and knock actually spell the word "ask." In the original Greek, those words are translated "keep on asking," "keep on seeking," and "keep on knocking." We are to persevere in prayer until we receive (verse 8). Verse 11 assures us that our heavenly Father will give good things to those who keep on asking.

The verses in Luke 11:10–13 are similar to the ones we just read in Matthew 7. What is different in verse 13?

____

____

____

How much more will God give *the Holy Spirit* to those who keep on asking! We will see on Day 5 the role of the Holy Spirit in prayer. Isn't it reassuring to know we can ask for more of His Spirit, more of His presence within us?

If Jesus tells us to ask, seek, and knock, then we are assured that our words to God matter. They will produce results. I hope you are encouraged to see the importance and power of your prayers, not only for yourself and your family, but for your community and nation as well. Ask, seek, knock—and don't quit!

Tomorrow we will look at various reasons to pray: for wisdom, for protection, and to resist temptation, just to name a few.

DAY 3: Reasons to Pray

My father served on a naval destroyer during WWII. When I was a young child, he took us to New York City to tour an enormous ship docked in the harbor. I remember standing next to one of the gigantic anchors that towered over me. It must have weighed tons. A ship that size needed more than one anchor to keep it from drifting from its position.

Perhaps your life has been smooth sailing up until now, but many people, like me, have weathered rough seas and storms. The most valuable lessons in my life have come through those hardships that were bathed in prayer. Prayer and God's Word have served as my anchor, keeping me from drifting into dangerous waters and keeping me close to the Captain of my ship. My relationship with the Lord has prevented me from capsizing many times. That relationship began, as I mentioned before, when a lawsuit drove me to read and pray Scripture verses every day.

There are many reasons to pray, but I believe one of the main reasons is to develop an intimate relationship with the Lord. Many of us grew up without a close, loving relationship with our earthly fathers. That often makes it difficult to relate to our heavenly Father. God can seem light-years away—at least that's what it was like for me.

My father worked such long hours in his pharmacy that we rarely spent time with him. Then he left when I was a young teenager. Consequently, I had no concept of a loving heavenly Father. Perhaps you have grown up in a similar environment or struggle with understanding and experiencing the Father's love. After all, how does one relate to a supernatural being who is invisible, who is called God the Father, if we haven't experienced love from an earthly father? I got so desperate that I began to search for verses like the ones below to heal the hole in my heart.

Read the following verses. Personalize them in your own words.

Romans 5:8

____

____

Zephaniah 3:17

____

____

1 John 3:1

____

____

Psalm 103:8

Simply reading those verses was not enough to convince me of God's love. I had to meditate on them—spend time quietly allowing the words to soak into my heart and soul. At times, I still need a refresher.

While knowing Scripture is wonderful and necessary, prayer allows us to *experience* God's presence. Prayer binds us together with Him. God created us to be His family. Without communication, families can fall apart. When we understand the depth of God's love for us, we feel safe and secure enough to talk to Him as a child would talk to a parent. We need to know we are loved by God in order to have confidence that He cares about every detail of our lives. We can then share our deepest hurts and needs with Him, knowing that God will not reject us.

What are we commanded to do according to 1 Thessalonians 5:17?

Rewrite Colossians 4:2 in your own words.

As we can see from these verses, to pray is to obey God. Rather than see prayer as a duty, let's embrace it as a privilege to partner with God to bring His kingdom to earth. As we will see in the coming weeks, prayer is not simply telling God a laundry list of our needs. It is a dialogue, a two-way street. God is inviting us to share our hearts with Him. And if we read His Word and meditate on it, He will share His heart with us.

Let's look at other reasons why prayer is so vital to our lives.

As a physician, I made dozens of decisions for my patients' well-being every day. My nine years of medical training equipped me to evaluate and treat medical issues with confidence. However, after eight years in private practice, the Lord impressed on my heart to quit working and become a stay-at-home mom. This lifestyle was completely different! The lawsuit had shaken my decision-making confidence to the core. I suddenly realized I had very little assurance in how to make wise decisions for my two precious, young children. What does 1 Corinthians 3:18–19 say about the world's wisdom?

I knew I needed God's wisdom if I hoped to raise children who would become godly, Christ-centered adults. I clung to the promise in James 1:5. Describe in your own words what that verse promises to you and me.

Verses 6–8 give a caveat that we need to pay close attention to if we want God's wisdom for our everyday decisions. Explain the warning below.

Over time, I began to trust that God would give me wisdom both through reading Scripture and through prayer. In week three, we will go over the fundamentals of praying so you will have confidence that you are not alone in making wise choices for yourself and your loved ones.

Another great reason to pray is found in Matthew 26:41. Write the verse below and underline where our weakness lies.

We can have all the best intentions in the world, but we do have an enemy of our souls who wants to wreak havoc in our lives, especially when we are tired—and raising children or working full-time can be quite tiring. We are exhorted to watch and pray to avoid falling into temptation. Our flesh is vulnerable.

That brings us to another reason to pray. When we do fail and give in to temptation, we can confess our sins and receive God's forgiveness. Instantly!

What assurance of forgiveness do we have in 1 John 1:9? Rewrite it in your own words.

Since I tend to be a perfectionist (and perhaps you are too), I have found Romans 8:1–2 to be very reassuring, especially if I am struggling with guilt over my mistakes. How does that verse resonate with you?

When the Lord impressed on my heart to quit my medical practice, my husband was not working full-time in his profession. We depended on my employment for most of our expenses. On the surface, this was the worst possible time to quit my job. I struggled for months before finally obeying God's call. My biggest fear—how would we survive financially. What does Philippians 4:19 promise us?

I knew God's promise in Philippians 4:19, at least I knew it in my *head*. Over the next decade or so, we would face many financial challenges. None of our needs were too small to escape His notice. It wasn't always easy, but God kept His promise to provide.

Two of the biggest challenges in my life that require prayer—lots of prayer!—are negative emotions and stressful situations. Fear, worry, and anxiety can creep in unnoticed or descend suddenly like a hailstorm. What does 1 Peter 5:7 exhort us to do?

I took that verse as a command. I had ample opportunity to cast my cares on Him, sometimes dozens of times per day! Often, I would send up a prayer like this:

> *Lord, I am really struggling with (emotion). I cast this care upon You and lay this situation at Your feet. Please quiet me with Your love. Grant me Your wisdom and Your peace. In Jesus' name, amen.*

The last reason for prayer that we will address today is for protection. We have an enemy, Satan, who wants to destroy God's children. We must be on guard for ourselves and our families daily. That doesn't mean living in fear. It means knowing how to protect ourselves from enemy attacks. We will go into more detail about prayers for protection in week four.

Tomorrow we will look at what Jesus has to say about prayer.

DAY 4: What Jesus Says About Prayer

"Prayer doesn't do any good."

Surprisingly, this statement was uttered by a professor at my son's top-notch Christian university.

"But we teach our kids to pray," conceded the professor.

Really? Why? If prayer is ineffective, why did he teach his children to pray? The more I pondered his claim that prayer doesn't do any good, the more I wondered. Had he been hurt because God didn't answer an important prayer the way he wanted Him to?

I was shocked at what the professor had said, but relieved that my son knew enough Scripture to know the truth that prayer is essential. Fortunately, this authority figure had no influence on my son's prayer life.

Sadly, some students in his class may not have had a firm foundation in their faith and might have been persuaded to stop praying. How many parents had sent their children to this highly regarded Christian institution assuming their child would be educated from a Christian worldview?

While people may have different opinions on prayer, Jesus made His thoughts on the subject quite clear. And whatever Jesus says about prayer comes straight from God the Father. Read John 14:9–11.

What does Jesus assure His disciples about the source of His teachings?

____

____

____

What statements in those verses affirm that Jesus and God are one spiritually?

____

____

____

What does Jesus say in John 14:7?

____

____

____

Jesus assures us that He and the Father are one. We can trust that what Jesus says is the Father's truth.

Unlike my son's professor, we want and expect our prayers to produce results. What does John 15:4 say we must do to bear fruit?

Jesus encourages us with a promise in verse 7. Write the verse below.

How does one abide in Christ so that the good fruit comes forth from our prayers? List three ways that are given in John 15:9–17.

Jesus also promises an extra bonus to receiving answers to our prayers. Read John 15:11 and summarize it below.

One day the disciples observed Jesus praying. When He was done, one of them asked Jesus to teach them how to pray. I am so glad that Jesus didn't make prayer complicated. The Lord's Prayer, as it has come to be known, can be found in Luke 11:1–4 and Matthew 6:9–13. Go ahead and read both passages. Notice how simple the language is.

As an introvert, I had a hard time ever wanting to pray out loud. What if I said something wrong? I'd much rather listen to someone else pray. But Jesus gave us an easy example to follow. List some of the things you notice that Jesus prayed for.

I love to pray the Lord's Prayer. For me it's like a template that I can add to. For example, I might add, "Give us this day our daily bread—the bread of Your presence." Or "I want Your will, Your way." It's a good starting point if you are uncomfortable or self-conscious about praying.

In Luke 18:1 Jesus exhorts His disciples to pray and not give up. Some of my prayers have taken a decade or more to be answered, but the results were worth the wait. Jesus also warned people what to avoid when praying. Read Matthew 6:5–8. What does Jesus tell us not to do?

____

____

____

Prayer is not a spectator sport. It is not meant to draw attention to ourselves, but to be spoken with sincerity from our hearts. Our prayers need not be long, eloquent, or flowery. Thank goodness!

Jesus attached some other conditions to our prayers. Read Matthew 21:18–22. What is required of us in order to have our prayers answered?

____

____

____

One other thing to consider avoiding is what I call "fear prayers." When we struggle with fear, we need to pray. But if the prayer focuses on all the things that could go wrong and their horrible consequences, we end the prayer feeling worse than when we began. Rather than praying an encyclopedia's worth of negativity, we should focus on God. In doing so, we will leave our prayer time peaceful, hope-filled, and closer to Him.

Is there a certain time of day that is better to pray? While it is perfectly fine to pray at any time, I personally like to start my day with prayer. When my kids were little, I tried to be sure I read a short passage of Scripture before going downstairs to breakfast. Then we prayed together before heading off to school.

Now that my children are adults, I still start my day with prayer, but it's after I eat breakfast. Exercise perks up my brain and helps me focus, so I pray while walking the treadmill and then finish up my prayer time afterwards.

Before I experienced the power of prayer, I used to pray only at bedtime, mostly confessing all the mistakes I made that day. It wasn't uplifting. When the lawsuit hit, I had to start the day with Scripture and prayer to prepare spiritually and emotionally for what lay ahead. Putting God first prepared me to depend on Him throughout the day. I had fewer mistakes to confess at bedtime that way. Now prayer is so vital I find myself praying when driving, shopping, or doing something mundane. In Mark 1:35, when did Jesus pray?

____

____

____

In Luke 6:12, when and how long did Jesus pray? What was He about to do the next day?

____

____

____

Jesus spent the entire night praying before choosing His twelve disciples. He needed to know His Father's will as those men would be world changers. We know that Jesus only did and said what He saw and heard God say and do, so prayer was a vital part of Jesus' life to accomplish God's purpose in His earthly life.

We see a glimpse of how Jesus prayed in Hebrews 5:7. Describe it in your own words below.

____

____

____

Here we see Jesus' humanity and His emotions freely expressed. He did not shy away from being transparent when He prayed. We don't need to put on a good face to come to the Father. He accepts us in whatever state we are in mentally or emotionally.

In John 16:23–24, what does Jesus promise His disciples they can do after He is crucified and returns to heaven?

____

____

____

Jesus makes an exclusive claim in John 14:6. Rewrite it in your own words below.

When we pray in Jesus' name, we acknowledge that no one approaches the Father except through Christ. We are given an assurance in Hebrews 10:19–22. What confidence do believers have when we pray and why?

That passage comforts me. We can feel safe bringing any concerns to God in prayer.

Have you ever prayed for something for weeks, months, or years and given up on seeing that prayer answered? Write your thoughts and feelings below.

Prayers are not always answered immediately. We can easily become discouraged when we do not see results or if our prayers are not answered in the way we would prefer. When I committed my life to Christ, I was applying to medical school. Amazing answers to my prayers occurred rather quickly. But as I matured in my faith, many answers were slower in coming to pass as God stretched my faith muscles—and it hurt. I wanted to go back to the quick answer stage of my Christian walk. Maybe you can relate. What encouragement does Jesus give us in Luke 18:1–5?

I don't want to be someone who walks into an office, takes a ticket, waits for the number to be called, but then walks out right before that number comes up. Do you? Jesus said never give up. We have to learn to trust God's timing, even when it frustrates us.

When our children were small and impatient about seeing their prayers answered, I would have them imagine sitting in a theater with the curtains closed, waiting for the show to begin. I would tell them, "God is getting everything ready behind the scenes. He has to get the right people in the right places and arrange everything first. When it's all ready, we will see the curtain go up, and our prayer will be answered." Even today, that picture helps me when I grow impatient with what seems to be a delayed answer to my request.

Lastly, we see Jesus' profound love for us as He prays to the Father right before His arrest and crucifixion. Read John 17. Starting at verse 6, list what Jesus asks the Father to do for His disciples after His resurrection.

____

____

____

Did you catch the verse that includes you in these promises? In verse 20, Jesus applies His prayer to all who will believe in the future. That's you and me!

If you ever struggle with whether God loves you, reread chapter 17. Focus on how much the Father and Son love you! They long to hear from you.

We will talk about many ways to pray in week three. Don't get caught up in looking for a formula. Prayer is all about connecting with God on a heart level and forging a close relationship with Him based on love.

Tomorrow we will look at the role the Holy Spirit plays in our prayer life.

DAY 5: The Holy Spirit's Role in Prayer

"Gold Mania" read the headline in an 1848 newspaper regarding the California gold rush. John Marshall began the stampede when he discovered gold flakes in the American River that runs through the Sierra Nevada Mountains. Thousands of would-be prospectors hurried to the West Coast to pan for gold.

For me, prayer is like panning for gold. I love to sit and talk to the Lord and sift the Scriptures for nuggets that are waiting for me to find them.

As Jesus prepared His disciples for His crucifixion and return to heaven, He promised them a priceless gift worth more than gold—the Holy Spirit.

In John 16:7, Jesus explains the necessity of leaving them. What is His reason as stated in that verse?

____

____

____

Jesus calls the Holy Spirit "the Counselor." What other name does He use in verse 13 to refer to Him?

____

____

____

When the Apostle Paul prays for the believers in Ephesus, he prays that God will give them the Spirit of wisdom and revelation (see Ephesians 1:17).

What are two of the best things to pray for? Wisdom and a teachable heart. That is at the heart of this Bible study: learning how to pray for wisdom and how to hear God's responses so you can position yourself in the center of His will. His wisdom is so precious—we don't want it to fall on deaf ears.

When I pray, I am panning for golden nuggets of God's wisdom. I want to make the best choices for myself and my family. I resonated with Jesus' statement to His disciples in John 15:5 (NIV): *Apart from me you can do nothing.* I have felt that way thousands of times. I need Jesus every day.

Perhaps you struggle with making wise choices in your career, your relationships, or your finances. By the end of this study, you too will know how to pan for God's gold.

In the Old Testament, we see examples of the Holy Spirit coming upon certain individuals. In Deuteronomy 34:9, Moses had just died prior to the Israelites crossing into the Promised Land, and Joshua became their leader. Summarize verse 9 below:

Joshua had big sandals to fill in taking the place of Moses. The spirit of wisdom that Moses carried was imparted to Joshua by the laying on of hands.

In 1 Samuel 10:1, Saul had been anointed by Samuel to be the first king of the Israelites. In verse 6, Samuel tells Saul that the Spirit of the Lord will come upon him in power, and he will be changed into a "different person."

These examples foreshadow the outpouring of the Holy Spirit at Pentecost. After His resurrection, Jesus appeared to the disciples over a forty-day period. What does Jesus instruct the disciples to do in Acts 1:4, right before He ascends into heaven?

In Acts 1:8, what does Jesus tell them about that gift?

Jesus had already told them that He had to go away in order to send the Counselor, also called the Spirit of wisdom. Then He told them the Holy Spirit will empower them to spread the gospel to the nations. This would fulfill the prophecy in Joel 2:28 that God would pour out His Spirit on all flesh. Instead of just a few individuals, all believers in Christ receive the Holy Spirit when we make Jesus our Lord and Savior (see Acts 2:38).

In the Old Testament, God's Spirit rested on those He anointed. In the New Testament, we learn that the Holy Spirit lives within all believers. Write 1 Corinthians 3:16 below.

Because we are assured that the Holy Spirit lives in us, all Christians have access to God's truth and wisdom 24/7! We are never going to receive a busy signal when we pray. We are never placed on hold. I would much rather rely on His wisdom than my own, so I frequently ask the Holy Spirit to guide my decisions.

I can't overemphasize the uniqueness of God's gift to us. The Holy Spirit plays many roles in our lives. What are two things that God's Spirit does when we pray as stated in Romans 8:26?

God's Spirit empowers us to live godly lives. We don't have to rely on our own strength. In fact, the Scriptures say that His strength is made perfect in our weakness (see 2 Corinthians 12:8–9). Many times I feel inadequate for a task, and I find myself calling on the Holy Spirit to empower me to do what God requires of me.

Jesus' ministry lasted approximately three years. I wonder if the disciples felt it was way too brief to learn all they needed to know to spread the gospel to the nations. Even Jesus seemed to indicate that. What does He say to them in John 16:12?

His time on earth was ending, but Jesus would not leave His followers helpless. He knew they would need God's Spirit every day. I love verse 13. Copy the first sentence and think about what an incredible gift that is.

What other promises are in that same verse? Write them below in your own words.

Jesus assured them that whatever the Spirit shares with the disciples will come from the Father. Verse 13 also tells us that God's Spirit will tell us of "things to come."

Does that intrigue you like it does me? I have only had that happen a few times, but I was filled with awe and wonder. My daughter has had that happen several times. Here's one example:

> After our daughter graduated from college, she was not sure what direction to take. After several months, she finally applied to clean cottages at a Christian retirement village. I really struggled with her decision. We paid all that money for college tuition just to have her vacuum and dust? By God's grace, I kept my mouth shut and prayed. About six weeks later, a position opened for an activities coordinator with the elderly residents. She had longed to work with the elderly since ninth grade, so this was her ideal job.
>
> Months later she let me in on her decision-making process. She had prayed and felt led to apply for the housecleaning position with an impression from the Lord that by taking that job another, better position would soon open at the same location. It was a great example of the Spirit telling her of "things to come."

Read John 14:26 to find several more attributes of the Holy Spirit related to prayer. Write the verse below.

____

____

____

Some translations of that verse use the word *Comforter* instead of Counselor. Just yesterday I was very upset, so I asked the Holy Spirit to be my Comforter. I inquired whether there was a Scripture that might bring comfort to me. Psalm 5 came to my mind, although I had no idea what was in that psalm. I found much comfort as I read those verses.

John 14:26 says that the Holy Spirit will remind us of what Jesus has said. I have found that at other times when I'm distressed, the Holy Spirit will bring to my attention a verse that I have memorized. Jesus is called the Word, so when a Scripture comes to mind it is akin to Jesus reminding me of what He has said.

Do you ever get discouraged? Here are encouraging words to pray in Romans 15:13. Write them below.

____

____

____

I often ask for His joy and peace so that the Holy Spirit will fill me to overflowing with hope.

To conclude this day's lesson, I want to encourage you with these verses from 1 Corinthians 2:10–12 (NIV). Let them soak into your spirit.

> *The Spirit searches all things, even the deep things of God. For who knows a person's thoughts except their own spirit within them? In the same way no one knows the thoughts of God except the Spirit of God. What we have received is not the spirit of the world, but the Spirit who is from God, so that we may understand what God has freely given us.*

The Holy Spirit searches the deep things of God. You and I have received that same Holy Spirit. He dwells within each of us. So we have access to those deep things as we seek Him with all our hearts, as we listen to Him, and as we trust Him and obey. What an awesome gift Jesus gave us!

Next week, we will begin by discussing the role that faith has in our prayers.

Because we are assured
that the
HOLY SPIRIT
LIVES IN US,
all Christians have
access to God's
truth and wisdom
24/7!

We are
NEVER GOING TO RECEIVE
A BUSY SIGNAL
when we pray.

TICKET:
PASSPORT

WEEK TWO

DAY 1: The Role of Faith in Prayer

Destination: Thailand

A small group of high school teens, including my daughter, were checking in at the Delta ticket counter for their ten-day mission trip to Thailand. The group then headed toward the security checkpoint—all but two of the girls.

The mother of Sarah (not her real name) approached me highly distraught. The airline refused to issue boarding passes to Sarah and one other girl because their passports would expire in less than six months after they returned home.

"You've got to pray for a miracle," she urged. Not only would the girls lose the travel experience but also the entire cost of the trip. Her daughter had worked hard to raise the money. To lose it would be devastating. The mom's desperation was palpable.

How much faith did I have to pray that a major airline would bend its rules for two teenagers? In that moment, none. Absolutely none. All I had was compassion for the two girls and the mom who looked at me with tears in her eyes and despair on her face. How could I not pray? We joined hands and asked God to get those girls on that flight.

Then I sat down next to the other young lady to console her while she waited for a ride home. Meanwhile, Sarah had gone back to the counter to talk with an agent, and the rest of the group headed to the gate. Another agent joined the first, and before long, what had been impossible a moment before became reality. The supervisor overrode the first agent and issued the girls boarding passes. They ran to the gate and made the flight at the last minute. That's the power of prayer!

Read Mark 10:14. What did Jesus say to His disciples?

____

____

____

Young children by nature trust their parents and authority figures. We call that childlike faith. Jesus said what is available in God's kingdom is available to those who come to Him with the faith of a child.

Against all odds, Sarah pursued her boarding pass with childlike faith, and the Kingdom of God responded.

I also saw Proverbs 3:5–6 being played out by her mother. Summarize those verses below.

____

____

____

While I was processing the situation with logic and reasoning, Sarah's mother was trusting the Lord with all her heart. My reasoning blocked me from having any faith. But listening to the mother's plea produced compassion and the tiniest little bit of faith to pray—a mustard-seed-sized faith.

Our topic today is faith. Let's look at some examples from Scripture. In Matthew 17:20 (NIV), Jesus is responding to His disciples who wondered why they could not heal a little boy who had epilepsy. Jesus answered them: *Because you have so little faith. Truly I tell you, if you have faith as small as a mustard seed, you can say to this mountain, "Move from here to there," and it will move. Nothing will be impossible for you.*

Faith moves mountains because faith moves God.

Sarah's childlike faith, her mother's trust in the Lord to do the impossible, and my little mustard seed faith moved that airline mountain out of the way.

Let's look at the faith of the centurion who came to Jesus, pleading with Him to heal his paralyzed servant. Read Matthew 8:5–13. Jesus offered to go to the centurion's home to heal the servant. What surprising things did the centurion say to Jesus in verses 8–9? Summarize below.

____

____

____

Jesus marveled at the centurion's faith in His miraculous healing power. He responded to such faith by saying in verse 10: *Truly I tell you, I have not found anyone in Israel with such great faith* (NIV).

Faith is the conduit for God's power to be released. Hebrews 11:6 says that without faith we cannot please God. Jesus challenged His disciples with this statement in Luke 18:8 (NIV): *When the Son of Man comes, will He find faith on the earth?*

God is looking for those who will walk by faith and not by sight (see 2 Corinthians 5:7). Faith activates the hand of God. Faith is not blind—it rests on the foundation of God's Word. The more we know and understand Scripture, the more we know God's character. The more we nurture an intimate relationship with the Lord through prayer, the more our faith grows—from a mustard-seed-size faith to mountain-moving faith.

I have learned that faith requires action. When at a loss for what to do, I turn for encouragement to 2 Chronicles 20:1–24.

Summarize the impossible situation King Jehoshaphat and the Israelites were facing.

____

____

____

How did the king and the people respond to the threat of attack?

____

____

____

When desperate, we can call out to the Lord with the same plea that King Jehoshaphat cried: *"We do not know what to do, but our eyes are on you"* (2 Chronicles 20:12, NIV).

I love the Lord's gracious and merciful response. Write His answer to their prayers from verse 15.

____

____

____

In verse 16, the Lord revealed exactly where the enemy would attack, but the Israelites would not have to fight. They were to face the army, but the Lord would fight the battle for them. The king said, *Have faith in the LORD your God and you will be upheld* (verse 20, NIV). He then appointed men to go in front of the Israelite army to sing and praise the Lord.

Evidence of the Israelite's faith in God's promise was seen in their actions. As they sang and worshiped the Lord, what happened to the opposing army, as told in verses 22–23?

____

____

Contrast the Israelite army's faith with that of Gideon's. Gideon also felt helpless as the Midianites were stealing his people's harvest year after year. Read Judges 6:14–16. Summarize the conversation between the Lord and Gideon below.

Despite Gideon's claim to be too weak to fight, the Lord promised Gideon that He would be with him and give him victory. Read Judges 7:1–23. The Lord instructed Gideon to pare down his army from tens of thousands to a mere 300 men. What was His reason for doing this as stated in verse 2?

God alone received the glory when a 300-man army miraculously defeated over 135,000 of the enemy's men (see Judges 8:10).

Sometimes God fights our battles, and other times He tells us how we are to fight. In both cases, He is always with us no matter who is doing the fighting. In each instance, faith is expressed with action: praise and worship in the account of King Jehoshaphat and obedience to God's battle strategy in the account of Gideon.

When we pray, we need to ask what our part is in seeing the Lord answer our prayers. If it's finances, do we look for another job? Or is the Lord leading us to ask for a raise or cut our expenses? If it's a relationship issue, do we need to confront someone, or is the Lord impressing on our hearts that He will intervene, and our part is to pray, keep silent, and thank Him?

The importance of faith is emphasized in Hebrews 3:16–19. These verses refer to the account of Moses sending twelve men to scope out the land God promised them after their exodus from slavery in Egypt (see Numbers 13—14:25). The Israelites wandered for forty years in the desert because they believed the ten spies who declared it would be impossible to take the land.

What reason does Hebrews 3:19 give for the failure of the Israelites to enter the Promised Land?

Hebrews 4:2 (NIV) further explains: *The message they heard was of no value to them, because they did not share the faith of those who obeyed.*

The Israelites would have been spared forty years of wilderness wanderings and entered the Promised Land in a very short time if they had placed their faith in God's promise.

We need to knit together our faith and God's words to us in order to receive His promises and experience the power of prayer.

How important is faith? When Jesus visited his hometown of Nazareth and taught in the synagogue, many who heard Him questioned His authority. Read Matthew 13:53–58. Summarize verse 58 below.

____

____

____

Jesus did plenty of miracles in many towns, but He was blocked from doing them in His hometown because of unbelief or lack of faith. He was just a carpenter's son in their eyes, not the Son of God.

At times I have had great faith and other times little or none. Romans 10:17 tells us that we acquire faith by hearing the Word of God. That is why not only reading but also *listening* to Scripture is vital to build our faith. I have found that reading verses out loud has more impact on my faith than silent reading; hearing the words highlights things I may have glossed over by simply reading. For that reason, I have included an appendix at the end of the study with personalized faith-building Scriptures that I enjoy declaring.

Faith is a choice. Faith requires action. Faith tugs at God's heart and grabs His attention. Faith releases His power.

Many times, our situations and the evil that pervades the earth can be very disheartening. Record 1 John 5:4 below.

____

____

As believers in Christ, we are to live our lives as overcomers. That does not mean we will never have trials and testing. Hebrews 11 records numerous accounts of trials that were overcome by faith. By faith Sarah conceived at age 90 and gave birth to Isaac. By faith the walls of Jericho came down.

When my faith wavers, I personalize a portion of Hebrews 6:12 and speak it over myself: "I put my trust and confidence in God's power, wisdom, and goodness." I build my faith by speaking His words over my situation, by remembering what God has already done in my life, and by taking my eyes off my circumstances. It is not always easy, but it is worth fighting the fight of faith (see 1 Timothy 6:12).

My hope is that as you progress through this study, you will be buoyed up by the testimonies and Scriptures in each lesson, so that your faith becomes an anchor to your soul and lifts you above your circumstances.

Tomorrow we will discover what happens when we make prayer a priority.

DAY 2: Prayer, Priorities, and Provision

Prayer was not always a priority for me, nor was God. I had to learn the hard way. Until the lawsuit, my life was not focused primarily on the Lord but on the intensity of a challenging profession and the raising of two small children. We attended church regularly, and I prayed before seeing patients and then again right before dropping exhausted into bed. However, my priorities fell short of what God desired for me. Read Matthew 6:25–33. What does verse 33 say our priority ought to be?

____

____

____

When prayer is a priority, provision is promised. Sometimes we get that backwards. If we are stressed about finances, we may start focusing solely on our needs instead of the Lord. Jesus knew we would be anxious about many things. List the concerns He mentions in Matthew 6:25.

____

____

____

Jesus was speaking to a large crowd, telling them not to be worried about the basic necessities of life like food, drink, and clothing. What does He tell us in verse 32?

____

____

____

We are assured that God knows our needs. When we seek Him first, He takes care of those necessities. It is easy to fall prey to worrying about tomorrow and the next day. But what does Jesus say in verse 34?

____

____

____

Worrying may be a struggle for many of us. It takes discipline and practice to keep our focus on today and on God's promises. Sometimes I have to remind myself that

God provided just enough manna for each day when the Israelites wandered in the wilderness.

Over the years of being a stay-at-home mom, I experienced many instances of God's provision. The Lord led me to quit my career right in the middle of the malpractice suit. My husband was working a minimum-wage job while looking for employment in his profession. Money was tight. The Lord certainly had my undivided attention. I was right where He wanted me to be...and it was uncomfortable. Very uncomfortable. Would God provide? What promise does God give us in Psalm 145:15–16?

____

____

____

God's provision became my reality day after day, year after year through several periods of my husband's unemployment. Things might have been tight, but we never lacked. I remember driving to a prayer group Christmas brunch asking the Lord if I should return the gifts I had purchased for my children. My heart was heavy with financial burdens. Later, as I was walking out the door to go home, one of the women stepped outside and handed me an envelope.

"The Lord led me to give this to you," she explained.

I opened the envelope and was stunned to see $100 tucked inside! Enough money to pay for the children's gifts.

Experiencing a need or lack gives the Lord an opportunity to show up in surprising ways, and our faith grows exponentially. Often in the wilderness times of our lives, we see His hand move in amazing ways.

If you are struggling right now, I encourage you to seek the Lord diligently. Make Him your top priority. His mercies and grace are new every morning, just like the manna. It also helps to remember that the majority of things we worry about never come to pass. We could save much wasted time and stress by taking Jesus at His Word.

One way to put God first is by making prayer of prime importance. God has shown up in unusual ways when I have prayed about very small things, like timing. I have learned over the years that if it matters to me, it matters to Him. He is a gracious, loving heavenly Father. He is not bothered or offended by our requests.

Years ago we drove to a state park lodge for several days of relaxation on the kids' spring break. On the way there we had passed a go-kart place—one of our favorite things to do. We were all excited. After putting our things away, I suggested, "Let's pray about when to go."

The look on one child's face told me I was being way too spiritual. Total silence. Clearly I was on my own.

Lord, what would be a good time for us to go go-karting? I quieted my mind and sat and waited in silence. An impression came. One o'clock.

We arrived at 1 p.m. and had a blast racing around the track, then playing some of the pinball machines. By that time we were a bit hungry, but I noticed the snack bar was closed.

"Is it too early in the season to open the snack bar?" I asked the man in charge.

"Actually, we're not open," he responded. "We're just here for this birthday party. We don't officially open for another few weeks."

I was stunned. Had I assumed we could ride at any time any day, we would have missed this fun opportunity. I am convinced that the Holy Spirit must have prompted me to pray, knowing that the go-kart place would only be open for a few short hours on that particular day.

On another occasion the children and I were driving home from school on a Monday and passed a stand of Christmas trees. We stopped to pick one out, but neither child liked *any* of the trees.

Back in the car, I suggested we pray about where we could find a nice tree. A nearby family-owned farm came to mind, but neither child wanted to go. "Can we just go home?" complained a voice from the back seat. The sour looks on their faces told me there was no point making an ordeal of something that should be fun.

"Well then, let's pray for what day to go." Wednesday came to mind. That made no sense. My daughter had a meeting after school that day. *Hmm...maybe I got that wrong.* Oh well. When I picked up the children on Wednesday, my daughter cheerfully announced that her meeting had been cancelled. The tree hunt was on! We had a great time walking through the forest of trees and selecting one that everyone agreed to. When it came time to pay, the cashier told us the tree was 40 percent off. Out of curiosity I asked when the trees went on sale. "Yesterday," she replied.

Had we gone on Monday, we would have paid full price. God knew how to bless us with a bargain! Many times what does not make sense initially makes perfect sense after seeing the end results of praying.

Prayer has become a priority for me because I have seen its power in my life and my family's lives time and time again.

These so-called serendipities taught me a lot about the priority of prayer. Although I love saving time, I'm not obsessive in praying about it. However, I will pray about God's timing when I need to go somewhere where appointments aren't taken: a walk-in hair salon or early voting, for example. It has saved me from waiting in line many times. What does Psalm 145:18 say?

Remember what Jeremiah 29:13 promises us? If we want to know God intimately, we must seek and search for Him with all our hearts. We can be well-versed in Scripture and recite verses left and right, but still not know God personally. That is the goal of this study—knowing God on a deeper, more personal level.

Read John 5:39–40. Why was Jesus criticizing the Pharisees?

The Pharisees searched the Scriptures as an end in itself and failed to see that Jesus was the One the Scriptures pointed to as the Messiah. We need to be knowledgeable of God's Word, but mere head knowledge alone limits us. Head knowledge coupled with heart knowledge, however, has unlimited potential. We will talk more about this in week three.

What does the Apostle Paul urge believers to do in Colossians 4:2?

He says something similar in Romans 12:12. Write that verse below.

The above verses are summarized in 1 Thessalonians 5:16–18 (NIV): *Rejoice always, pray continually, give thanks in all circumstances; for this is God's will for you in Christ Jesus.*

week 2 day 2

Paul urged Christians to persist in prayer and to be hopeful and patient. Sometimes that feels like a tall order, especially the patience part. Paul knew the importance of praying as his life often depended on it.

Years ago a woman from Africa visited one of my friends. Commenting on her necessity to rise early and pray every morning, she said to my friend, "In Africa, if we don't pray, we don't eat."

Daily sustenance might not be as big a prayer priority to some of us; however, we may struggle in other areas: anxiety, depression, family rifts. Whether the issue is big or small, receive encouragement from Philippians 4:6–7. Write the verses below.

____

____

____

Paul urged Christians to pray in every situation so that God's peace would protect our hearts and minds. If something is stressing us out, we are wise to follow God's guidance to receive His peace that transcends all understanding.

Let's consider one last reason to make seeking the Lord in prayer a priority. What does Jesus promise His disciples in Matthew 11:28–30? Write the verses below.

____

____

____

When we seek the Lord, no matter what our circumstances are, He will give us rest for our souls. We are invited to give Him our burdens and to yoke ourselves to Him. We do that through prayer.

Let's finish today's lesson with one more promise for those who make the Lord a priority. Isaiah 26:3 (NIV) says: *You will keep in perfect peace those whose minds are steadfast, because they trust in you.*

Learning to trust and focus on God, not the problem, has been an ongoing process for me. In every trial and testing, I have chosen to depend on the Lord, delve deeper into the Scriptures, and make a conscious choice to trust Him with the outcome. We must learn to see our dependence on the Lord as a strength, not a weakness.

Tomorrow we will look at prayer and God's promises.

DAY 3: Prayer and Promises

Years ago a friend called asking for prayer about a job opportunity. She was seeking the Lord's wisdom about whether to accept an offer. From all *outward* appearances, the job seemed like a great fit.

As we prayed, I felt a strong heaviness in my spirit. I sensed there were unsavory things hidden from view that weren't obvious in her interview. I had no clue what they were but warned her. She turned down the offer. Additional information surfaced weeks later that confirmed she had made the right decision.

The Scriptures overflow with promises related to prayer. Let's start with wisdom, which is exactly what God gave my friend and me when we prayed about her job opportunity.

Our wisdom is limited and imperfect. God's wisdom is limitless and perfect. He sees what is hidden, knows what lies ahead, and wants to protect us. Whose wisdom would you prefer?

What two things does Proverbs 2:6 say we will get when we seek God's wisdom?

____

____

____

Wisdom, knowledge, and understanding are like a three-fold cord. We may have facts (knowledge) about our situation, but without understanding, those facts and how to apply them (wisdom) would be useless to us. God's wisdom is key to living an abundant life.

When uncertain about what direction to take, I often pray this prayer based on Jeremiah 42:3, "Lord, show me the way I should walk and the thing I should do." God has always been faithful to provide wisdom when I ask.

What does 2 Corinthians 1:20 tell us about God's promises?

____

____

____

Isn't it reassuring to know that God's promises are guaranteed? His promises are yes and amen.

It is frustrating to pray and not see an immediate answer. We can be tempted to think God has not heard us, or He is too busy with more important matters.

What does 1 Peter 3:12 tell us about His availability?

He is *always* listening to our prayers. God does not take vacations or have limited office hours. He neither slumbers nor sleeps (see Psalm 121:3–4). He cares about the smallest details of your life. You can talk to Him about *anything*.

What words in Psalm 33:13–14 reassure you that God is always aware of you?

Read Proverbs 15:3 and summarize it below.

God is well aware of us no matter where we are and no matter what our circumstances are. We may have to wait for His answers, but some of the most important prayers take the longest to be fulfilled.

When the Apostle Paul urges Christians to pray without ceasing (1 Thessalonians 5:17), Paul is not saying to pray 24 hours a day. He is encouraging believers not to give up praying if their prayers aren't answered immediately. Don't cease praying about what is on your heart. Trust in God's timing.

The following verses encourage me to persevere in prayer. First John 5:14–15 (NIV) says:

> *This is the confidence we have in approaching God: that if we ask anything according to his will, he hears us. And if we know that he hears us—whatever we ask—we know that we have what we asked of him.*

If we ask according to God's will, we are guaranteed that He hears us. How do we know what that will is? We search the Scriptures to know what God has promised. God's Word is His will. We pray those promises back to Him. Then we can have confidence that He has heard our petitions.

As a new believer, I began to pray for my mother's salvation, assured from 2 Peter 3:9 that God wants everyone to be saved and spend eternity with Him. But every time I spoke with her about God, she rebuffed me with anger. More than thirty years later, she came to know the Lord five months before her death. Did I pray every single one of those days? No. The situation wasn't on my radar all the time, but clinging to God's promises and persisting in prayer finally paid off.

As a career person and then a parent, there were many times when I ran out of steam. Fatigue overwhelmed me. God promises in Isaiah 40:31 to renew our strength when we're weary if we wait on Him. Summarize that verse below.

____

____

____

When exhaustion took over, I would recite Isaiah 40:31 out loud and be refreshed. My prayer might sound like this: *"Lord, I place my confidence and hope in You. Please renew my strength so I will run and not get weary. I need extra grace right now to finish out this day."*

Ephesians 3:20 (NKJV) says that God is able to do *exceedingly abundantly above all that we ask or think.* I saw this promise played out when one of my tires kept losing air pressure. I prayed that it might just be a nail in the tire that could easily be patched. Indeed, the loss of pressure was due to a nail, but it could not be patched. I pulled out my credit card to pay for the new tire and was stunned to hear, "No charge." *What? How could that be?* The manager gave me a free tire simply because I was a regular customer. All the way home, I thanked the Lord for doing above and beyond what I asked for.

Read Mark 11:23–24 (NKJV). Jesus said to His disciples in verse 23:

> *Whoever says to this mountain, 'Be removed and be cast into the sea,' and does not doubt in his heart, but believes that those things he says will be done, he will have whatever he says.*

Jesus used the word mountain to symbolize hindrances or obstacles that need to be removed. He also said that we need to speak to that hindrance and not doubt in our hearts. When we pray in faith and believe God's promises, we can see the impossible become possible. Write what Jesus said in Mark 11:24 below.

____

____

____

My daughter faced a huge mountain blocking her way to the one university she hoped to attend. Going to college was not even on her radar when she was in middle school. However, while visiting a nearby university, she sensed the Lord indicating that that was where she would attend college.

During her senior year, she applied for early admittance but was denied. She then applied to other schools, received acceptances, but she was still convinced that the first school was her only choice. All senior year I prayed that God would open a door somehow and persisted in believing that she would be accepted.

The night before graduation at the baccalaureate service, each senior announced which college he or she would be attending in the fall. My daughter had no clue what to say until she stood in front of the microphone. I was astonished to hear her announce that she would be graduating from that university (despite not having been accepted)!

After graduation, the guidance counselor called us in to outline alternative means of admittance. My daughter chose to write a letter of appeal, and two weeks later was accepted. Perseverance and the power of prayer moved that mountain out of her way.

Are you facing a mountain right now, something that seems impossible? What did Jesus tell His disciples in Matthew 19:26? Write the verse below.

____

____

____

Whatever we focus on will magnify. If we emphasize the mountain, talk about the mountain, and complain about the mountain, it will grow bigger in our thoughts, making it seem impossible to move and more difficult to pray about in faith.

If we believe God's promises and declare God's power, faith will overshadow any doubts. Declarations are powerful faith builders.

Scripture urges us not to focus on that which is seen but rather on that which is unseen. That which is unseen is eternal, whereas that which we can see is only temporary (2 Corinthians 4:18). God's power is invisible, yet it is capable of moving mountains. Contending for my daughter's college acceptance was not easy; we fought doubts and discouragement for nine months. We had no clue how she would get in, but God knew. He wanted to grow our faith and trust in Him. Every test we go through is an opportunity to go deeper with the Lord and see the power of His promises.

Let's look at one more Scripture reference related to prayer before we close out this lesson. Read Psalm 91:14–15. There are six promises in those two verses. List the six below.

____________________	____________________
____________________	____________________
____________________	____________________

Now that we know some of the promises associated with praying, we will look at the cost of prayer tomorrow.

DAY 4: The Cost of Prayer

My fixation with time probably began in medical school. Was it an idol? I'm not sure, but I was very time conscious. I operated on warp speed to complete all the duties required on my shift. I was a type A medical Martha, focused on tasks to the exclusion of all else.

Although prayer is free, it will cost you certain things, and time is one of them. While we can pray anytime and anywhere, if we fail to set aside time to focus on talking and listening to the Lord, we will lose out on the most precious aspect of being a follower of Christ—a deep relationship with the Lord.

When I began my new career as a stay-at-home mom, one of the first things that had to go was my tight control of time. My focus on a to-do list had to decrease and my time with the Lord had to increase. I desperately needed His wisdom on how to raise godly children. There were no shortcuts to parenting. Setting aside time to pray became an essential.

I soon learned the costs of prayer included other things besides just time. Take sleep, for example. One of our children had a habit for years of popping out of bed and knocking on the bedroom door just as I was falling asleep. Anxious thoughts needed to be processed and prayed over, right then. Not the next morning. Prayer with this little one was more important than my sleep.

In addition to costing you time, prayer may bring division from people and even cost a friendship or two. Have you ever had to end a relationship with a family member or friend? Read Matthew 10:34–38. What does Jesus warn us about relationships?

____

____

____

Prayer brings us closer to the Lord, but as we mature in our faith and walk in obedience to the Lord's directions, friends or family members may not understand our choices.

Sometimes the Lord would lead me to make a decision that was at odds with the strong opinion of someone close to me. If our disagreement was irreconcilable, we would part ways. Obedience to God had to take precedence over the relationship, yet saying goodbye was still painful.

In Matthew 10:36 (NIV), Jesus says that *a man's enemies will be those of his own household.* What instructions did Jesus give the people on how to treat their enemies in Matthew 5:43–44?

____

____

____

Jesus wasn't saying they had to like what their enemy was doing or have warm, loving feelings for them. We can treat people with love and grace even when we do not agree with them. It isn't easy, especially if it's a family member or close friend.

Is there someone in your life that you find very difficult to treat with love? Write your thoughts below.

____

____

____

When I find myself in that situation, I struggle too. My prayer is usually, "Lord, love that person through me. Please give me Your compassion for them." I also pray that the Lord will show me what might be troubling them and causing them to act out toward me. It's easier to have compassion and pray when we have some understanding of their pain or struggles. Ask the Lord to help you see that person through His eyes. Ask for His grace to treat them with love and ask whether you need to set healthy boundaries.

Praying for our enemies may eventually change their hearts and their behaviors. It certainly can change ours. The results of our prayers for them are up to the Lord. Our job is to pray and obey.

Interruptions are another cost of prayer. When I go grocery shopping, I am very list oriented. I don't wander around browsing the shelves. One time as I headed out of the produce department, I noticed a woman had fallen. Her husband and another woman were attending to her. *Thank goodness*, I thought. I did not want to get involved.

But as I started to move on, I sensed that the Lord wanted me to get involved. What a struggle between obedience and my desire to finish my shopping! Even though two others were already helping, I couldn't erase the thought to go over and intervene. I parked my cart and walked over. To my surprise, a friend I had not seen in years was the shopper who was helping. I was blessed to reconnect with my friend and to pray for the woman before the paramedics arrived.

In Mark 5:21–34 we see how Jesus dealt with an interruption. What was Jesus doing when the woman with the issue of blood touched Him from behind?

Jesus was headed toward the synagogue ruler's home to heal his daughter. She was on the point of death, so it was imperative that He not delay. However, Jesus stopped when He felt power leave His body. He turned and addressed the woman who touched His clothes. Jesus wasn't angry at the interruption. He treated her with kindness.

What if I were that woman? Or the woman who fell in the grocery store? Wouldn't I want someone to sacrifice their time and be willing to have their life interrupted to pray for me? I need to be mindful that God is often in the interruptions if I will stay sensitive to His nudges.

Prayer may also cost us heartache and disappointment when our prayers are not answered the way we would like. Recently, I was asked to pray for a missionary couple I had never met. No matter how hard our church prayed, the husband died of an infection, leaving a young wife and handicapped daughter. I still pray for their hearts, and I struggle with not having any answer as to why God did not heal him.

Prayer will also cost us the pain of conviction. One day as I was driving, another car cut me off. I immediately said out loud, "Lord, just bless him." Just as quickly, I was convicted that my tone was sarcastic, and my attitude was one of irritation, not true blessing. I repented and prayed the prayer again, this time really meaning it. Ouch!

In Psalm 139:23–24, what does David ask God to do?

When David prayed, he asked the Lord to search his heart for any sin. Sin distances us from God. If we ask, He will show us what we need to confess and what wrongs we need to make right. It may be uncomfortable to have our hearts searched, but that process will draw us closer to our heavenly Father.

Prayer may cost us finances. Sometimes when I am praying, I feel a conviction to purchase something for someone or give a certain amount to a ministry. Having been raised by a very frugal Scottish mother in a single parent home, I have had to learn to trust God with finances, especially when giving sacrificially or when money seems tight. While I may sometimes struggle to obey, I always feel joy when I finally submit to the Lord's promptings.

Another cost of prayer is giving up the right to know why. Early on in my prayer journey, I found that asking God why something happened usually met with silence. Why did that young person die, or why is there so much evil? I have learned not to ask for the most part. That is one of the sacrifices of prayer, not always understanding but continuing to trust God and to pray regardless.

The cost of prayer may mean self-sacrifice: giving up a comfortable lifestyle, laying down one's career, or caring for a family member who has treated us poorly. Before I quit my medical practice, my husband and I were planning to build our dream home. After numerous forays looking at beautiful homes and talking to builders, I finally had no peace about it. I had no idea why. Months after we stopped looking, the Lord impressed on my heart to lay down my career. Only then did I understand why I had no peace about house hunting. Obedience may be required before we have complete understanding.

The cost of prayer also includes not seeing the results of what we are praying for. I often pray for souls to be saved in other nations. I also pray for the persecuted church around the world. I won't know the results of my time spent interceding until I get to heaven.

Read Matthew 6:10. This verse is part of the Lord's Prayer. Write the verse below:

____

____

____

At times we will have to lay down our will for His, when what we want or think is best for us is not God's will. It might even be a small sacrifice that seems trivial. I experienced this one Christmas as I planned to dress up for our church's annual Christmas pageant. When I stepped into my closet, I felt a surprising impression to wear jeans. *Jeans? To a festive occasion like this? Everyone will be wearing nice clothes*, I thought.

I tried to dismiss the thought, but it kept recurring. Reluctantly, I donned blue jeans and arrived early to sit where I would not be noticed. I happened to turn around just as a friend entered the sanctuary wearing jeans. She was not a member of our church, so I hurried up the aisle to welcome her.

"I'm so glad you are wearing jeans," she said with relief. "We were out shopping, and I really wanted to come to your Christmas show, but we didn't have time to go home and change clothes." What a loving heavenly Father, who wanted my friend to feel accepted and asked me to be a small part of that.

Jesus made the ultimate sacrifice of His will on the cross. Read Matthew 26:36–42. As Jesus prays in the Garden of Gethsemane, what does He say to God in verse 39? Write the verse below.

____

____

____

Jesus expressed extreme grief and sorrow knowing He was about to be arrested and crucified. He came to earth to pay the price for our sins by becoming the perfect sacrifice. He was fully human and fully God. His human nature agonized over what lay ahead of Him, yet He surrendered His will to that of His Father.

When we pray, it is important to yield our will to God's. Yielding can be a real struggle at times, especially when we cannot understand the significance of what He is asking us to do. I argued and reasoned with God for several months before laying down my career. In retrospect, that decision was the best one I could have made for our family, but it looked just the opposite at the time.

Prayer has its costs, but the benefits always far outweigh them. Jesus came to give us an abundant life, and prayer is how we access that abundance (see John 10:10). I used to think prayer was just reading off my laundry list of requests, but I have learned there are various types of prayer. We will look at those tomorrow.

DAY 5: Types of Prayer

As a new believer in Christ, I felt like I was fighting one battle after another, especially in medical school. With no time to do Bible studies and knowing very little Scripture, sometimes all I could manage were simple "Help me, God!" prayers. They carried me through for a season, but God wanted more of me, and I needed more of Him. To develop a deeper relationship with the Lord, I needed to learn different types of prayer.

When our children were little, I taught them to pray using Psalm 100:4 as our starting point. Children love stories of kings, so I had them imagine God as a king in a castle complete with a courtyard and gate. Read Psalm 100:4, and write it below.

____

____

____

The key to having an audience with our heavenly King is through thanksgiving and praise. Thanksgiving gives us entrance through the gates, and praise allows us into His courtyard. We started our prayers thanking God and praising Him before we presented any requests. Then we again thanked Him for hearing and answering our prayers before saying amen.

Have you ever struggled with being thankful? Has it ever been difficult to praise God during trying times? Write your thoughts below.

____

____

____

Read Hebrews 13:15 and summarize below.

____

____

____

When nothing seems right, we may struggle to praise God. Our emotions may be shouting, "Why is this happening to me?" or "When will this end?" Our feelings are in a turmoil, and all our thoughts are negative. Praise during trials may seem unnatural, but God sees it as a beautiful sacrifice (see Jeremiah 33:11).

On particularly difficult days, when my world has turned upside down, I find comfort in reading Psalms.

Read Psalm 142. David is hiding in a cave and crying out to the Lord in desperation regarding his foes. Describe some of his complaints below.

David felt persecuted and overwhelmed. His enemies were seeking to destroy him. When I compare my troubles to David's, my problems no longer seem as huge. What boosts my spirits is how he ends each psalm with something positive and uplifting. What does he say in the last verse (verse 7)?

David seems to be an eternal optimist. His psalms demonstrate that it's acceptable to pour out our hearts to God when we are in turmoil. He sets a good example of thanking and praising God at the end of his complaints, which is truly a sacrifice of praise.

When I wake up to a day that I am not looking forward to, when the things on my to-do list are not inviting (a dentist appointment or a meeting with a tax accountant), I make a choice to speak Psalm 118:24 over myself before I even get out of bed. Write verse 24 below.

The fact that we wake up and have breath is something we can be thankful for even if we aren't looking forward to those appointments.

When I am especially desperate, I sometimes pray "planet prayers." By that I mean I start my prayer thanking and praising God for all the beautiful planets, galaxies, and stars that He created just for us. By forcing myself to focus on the majesty and grandeur of His universe and the awesome power it took to create it, I become encouraged. My problems then seem much smaller and manageable with His help. Reverence and awe quiet my anxiety and stress (see Hebrews 12:28).

In reality, God does not *need* our praise and thanksgiving. But He knows that when we enter His presence with grateful hearts, our spirits are lifted, and we are blessed by drawing closer to Him.

Besides thanksgiving and praise, there are other types of prayers, like prayers of agreement. What does Jesus say in Matthew 18:19?

Most of my prayers are offered up when I am alone with God. But when a mountain needs to be moved, I will call or text a friend to agree with me in prayer. You read a prayer of agreement example in the previous lesson with the airline incident. Being familiar with the Word of God is vital so that we do not agree in prayer about something that violates Scripture.

The early church frequently met together to pray in agreement. Read Acts 12:1–12. Summarize below.

Although four squads of soldiers were guarding Peter in prison, an angel came and set him free. Review verses 5 and 12. Write verse 5 below.

The constant prayers of the church released Peter from captivity through angelic intervention.

Although our prayer gatherings may not be as dramatic as the one for Peter, we can be assured that the Lord is in our midst and that He hears every prayer, even if we are "gathered" on the phone or the Internet.

One of the most powerful ways to pray is to declare God's Word over yourself, your family, and any situation that needs His intervention. Scripture declarations release the authority and power of God.

Read Job 22:27–28 and summarize the verses below.

Verse 28 in the Amplified translation states:

> *You will also decide and decree a thing, and it will be established for you;*
> *And the light [of God's favor] will shine upon your ways.*

We are assured that not only does the Lord hear our prayers, but we can declare His truths over our lives and light will shine on our ways.

Read Psalm 119:105 to discover what that light is.

Being familiar with Scripture and declaring it over your life illuminates your path going forward, especially when you are unsure which steps to take. God's Word is like a spotlight that protects you from any obstacles that might trip you up.

Here's an example of how I make Scripture declarations:

> *I shall decide and decree a thing, and the light of God's favor will shine upon my path. I declare I am more than a conqueror. I can do all things through Christ's strength today. My God will supply all my needs according to His riches in Christ. In Jesus' name, amen* (see Job 22:28, Romans 8:37, Philippians 4:13, Philippians 4:19).

Declaring Scripture is decreeing the will of God for your life and for those for whom you are interceding. It is a powerful way to build your faith and to dispel doubt or fear. (See Appendix A for more declarations.)

When we contend for something in prayer, we may get pushback from the enemy of our souls. This brings us to spiritual warfare prayers. What does 1 Peter 5:8 say about Satan? Write the verse below.

The devil does not want God's children to succeed, and he will sneak around trying to waylay us, especially right before we cross over a new threshold in our lives. What does John 10:10 say?

That verse describes the battlefield we live on. On one hand the enemy wants to destroy God's plans for our lives. On the other hand Jesus wants to bless us with abundant life. Read Ephesians 6:10–18. Who are we wrestling against?

Scripture makes it clear that our real enemy is not other people, but spiritual forces from the kingdom of darkness—Satan's domain. Those evil spirits may prompt certain people to come against us, but we are really in a spiritual battle of light versus darkness. Where does our power to fight this evil come from? Record verse 10 below.

Our power comes from the Lord. That is why declaring Scripture is so important as a protection. One of the verses I declare frequently is Isaiah 54:17 (NKJV): *No weapon formed against you shall prosper.* We have only touched briefly on spiritual warfare. We will learn more about prayers of protection in week five.

Our last type of prayer is probably the one we use most frequently—prayers of petition. Before learning about the importance of thanksgiving, declaring, agreement, and spiritual warfare, I simply listed my requests and finished with, "In Jesus' name, amen."

I really had no concept of developing a personal relationship with God. He seemed awfully far away. I had no idea that prayer was meant to be a dialogue, not a monologue. Think back to Adam and Eve in the Garden of Eden having two-way conversations with God. That is what He wants for you and me. Somehow it never occurred to me to give the Lord a chance to respond to my prayers.

We miss so much when we only present our list of needs to God. If we are seeking His wisdom, it's important to wait on His response. If nothing comes to mind, then I trust God will keep His promise to answer in His timing. Often the wisdom I am seeking comes as a thought while involved in a mundane task like folding the laundry, but I always want to leave room to hear from Him during my prayer time.

It's vital to honor God as our Creator, our heavenly Father. He is someone to be treated with reverence and awe. I'm afraid in the past there were many times I probably treated Him more like a vending machine or a genie in a bottle. I had not yet learned how to honor Him and put His will for my life first. I had to learn submission to His authority.

In week three we will go into more depth on the mechanics of prayer. Just a caution today not to look for a formula. When we talk with a family member or a close friend, we don't communicate in lists or formulas. We should speak the same way with God. We can just be ourselves. We can tell Him what concerns us, and we can learn to listen for His still small voice in response. This takes practice, but it is well worth the effort to pray from our hearts, not our lists.

WEEK THREE

DAY 1: Preparing to Pray with Power

Let's dive into the basics of praying with power. Praying should not be like placing an order on Amazon, but more like confiding in your closest friend. The Lord wants to be that friend.

To prepare our hearts for deep intimacy with Him we need passion, consecration, and reverence. These three keys enable us to receive personalized answers to our prayers.

During my residency in dermatology, I had a passion for popcorn. So much so that as I drove home from work, my mind was focused on eating a quick dinner, so I could then relax with a large bowl of buttery goodness. This was the highlight of my day—something I looked forward to especially when stressed. I hate to admit I had more of a hunger for popcorn than spiritual treasures. Read Matthew 6:19–21 and summarize below.

____

____

____

Jesus taught that earthly treasures disappear quickly; they are temporary (like popcorn!). But treasures stored in heaven last *forever*. Passionately pursuing a deeper relationship with the Lord reaps huge rewards on earth and in heaven.

When a Pharisee asked Jesus what the greatest commandment was, what did Jesus say in Matthew 22:36–37?

____

____

____

We need to love God with all our *hearts*, souls, and minds—to treasure Him. Just knowing Scripture in our heads does not equate to intimacy with Him, as we saw previously in John 5:39–40 when Jesus rebuked the religious leaders for refusing to recognize Jesus as the Messiah. In verse 42 (NKJV) Jesus further states, *But I know you, that you do not have the love of God in you.*

A relationship with the Lord requires both heart and head knowledge. God is drawn to passionate believers, those who delight to spend time in His presence and in His Word.

Are you satisfied with your relationship with God? If not, what would you like to improve?

Write Exodus 20:3 below.

Because of our fallen nature, we may find ourselves making a god of money, power, material goods, etc. Take a minute and ask the Lord if there is anything that is preempting Him in your life. Has He fallen out of first place in your life? Write your thoughts below.

If God showed you something, renounce its hold on you, ask for forgiveness, and release it to Him. God wants us to make Him our top priority, to treasure Him in our hearts.

Passion for Bible study and prayer did not come naturally to me. I spent weeks asking for a divine hunger for His presence and His Word before I began to feel excited about spending time reading Scripture and sitting in His presence. Now I look forward to discovering the nuggets of wisdom tucked into the pages of Scripture.

Here's a prayer you can pray if you need a jump start in your spiritual walk:

> *Lord, I want to be excited about spending time with You. Please ignite a fire in my spirit that burns with a desire to know You intimately. Give me a passion for Your presence and Your Word. In Jesus' name, amen.*

Pray it with all your heart and pursue God until you experience it.

Are there still days when I approach God more out of duty than zeal? Yes, but that's a warning that I need to stir up that fervor again.

Besides passion, we also need to consecrate ourselves to the Lord. Write 1 Corinthians 6:20 below.

____

____

____

We glorify God by living lives that line up with His Word and honoring Him in our hearts. What does the Apostle Paul tell us in Romans 12:2?

____

____

____

We are exhorted to be in this world but not of it and to be transformed by renewing our minds with Scripture. In Psalm 51:10 David prays to be consecrated. Write the verse below.

____

____

____

God called David a man after His own heart even though David committed some serious sins. We all sin and fall short of God's glory. The key to living a consecrated life is to repent quickly and then rededicate ourselves to the Lord whenever we fall short.

Let's consecrate our lives anew to the Lord before we further explore the fundamentals of praying powerful prayers.

> *Heavenly Father, I submit myself to You and come before You asking for Your will, Your way each and every day. I consecrate my life to You. Create in me a clean heart. Sanctify me by Your Word, and teach me Your ways that I might walk in them. In Jesus' name, amen.*

To experience the power of prayer, we not only need passion and consecration, but we also need reverence. Read Proverbs 9:10, and record the verse below.

____

____

____

The word *fear* in this verse means reverence, a holy awe of who God is. We are wise to come into His presence in prayer with deep honor and respect. We are not to be afraid of Him, but we highly esteem Him.

Passion, consecration, and reverence prepare our hearts for fellowship with the Lord. But what about our environment? How do we create a place to pray that is conducive to prayer?

When I began to pursue the Lord, I found that solitude and quiet were essential in order to eliminate distractions. It's all about location.

Jesus always retreated either to a mountain or a garden to pray alone (see John 17). Read John 5:19. What does Jesus say in this verse?

____

____

____

Jesus needed to know the Father's will *before* ministering and teaching. Prayer was a high priority for Him. If we want to know how to be in the center of God's will and make the best decisions, prayer is vitally important.

Find a quiet place with no distractions, even if it's a closet! If sitting still is difficult, try walking and praying. I do some of my praying while walking on a treadmill.

Keep a pen and paper handy. Often things to put on your to-do list will pop up in your mind when you start to pray. Write them down so you don't worry about trying to remember them later. It is also vital to silence your phone (even put it out of sight).

We need both a quiet place and a quiet mind. It was a big challenge for me to silence my thoughts and simply sit quietly in His presence.

Remember 1 Peter 5:7? We are exhorted to cast our cares on the Lord. If you are upset, tell the Lord how you feel. Then ask Him to quiet your soul (your mind, will, and emotions). The more you practice, the easier it becomes to have a quiet mind.

Here's a prayer I pray to get started:

> *Lord, I submit myself to You. Holy Spirit, please take control of my thoughts, my physical and spiritual senses, my emotions, my imagination, my memories, and my physical and spiritual body. Cause my thoughts and heart to agree with Yours. Surround me with Your presence. Take away any distractions.*

Read Romans 8:5 and summarize below.

____

____

____

As a left-brained thinker, I used to set my mind on my problems and how to solve them. It took practice to stop analyzing and to focus my mind on hearing from the Lord. I had to tell my flesh: **BE QUIET!**

Read 2 Corinthians 4:17–18. What are we encouraged to focus on?

____

____

____

The physical world makes it difficult to concentrate on the spiritual things that we cannot see. Focusing on problems magnifies them, making it harder to trust God's power and ability to intervene in our circumstances.

Whenever you struggle with what seems to be an insurmountable problem, try meditating on Matthew 19:26 (NKJV): *With men this is impossible, but with God all things are possible.*

There is no problem in your life that God cannot solve.

Left-brain thinkers tend to focus on logic and reasoning. We are so busy talking and analyzing in our heads that it's hard for the Lord to get a word in edgewise. I found that activating my right brain relaxes me. The more relaxed I am, the easier it is to hear what the Lord is saying. If this is something you struggle with, you can switch to a right-brain activity by sitting out in nature or letting your mind relax by listening to quiet, instrumental music.

Once we have established a quiet environment and a quiet mind, we need to position ourselves to receive God's wisdom. If we truly want His will, not ours, it's important to "get to neutral" first. Getting to neutral means laying down strong opinions and negative emotions and having a teachable heart and a mind open to any possibility that does not violate Scripture. Can you agree to do His will even if you are not sure what He might direct you to do? Remember Luke 11:2 (NKJV): *"Your will be done."*

Read Isaiah 55:9 and write the verse below.

> ____
> ____
> ____

God has unique ideas that are beyond our human wisdom. We don't want to box Him in by putting limits on Him. God may have a solution we haven't even thought of.

What if Joshua had figured out a game plan for conquering Jericho and simply asked God to bless it? What if King Jehoshaphat had decided the odds were so great against beating his enemies that he asked God, "Where can we hide out?" Both would have missed seeing the hand of God produce miraculous victories.

Recently, I had a monthly meeting to attend, but everything in me wanted to skip the meeting. All I could think about was staying home. Have you ever felt that way?

I was honest with God. "I *really* don't want to go, Lord."

I could not quiet my strong negative emotions, so I finally prayed, "Lord, I say yes to this meeting if You want me to go." Since I could not get to neutral, I added, "Align my thoughts and heart to agree with Your plans for me."

As I busied myself with other things, all the negative feelings slowly melted away, and I heard quietly in my spirit, "Be a light." That confirmed God's will, so off I went. At the end of the meeting, someone asked me privately to pray for lost loved ones, and another person thanked me enthusiastically for encouraging her. I drove home overflowing with gratitude that the Lord blessed others through me and blessed me to boot.

Saying yes is not always easy at first, but remember that God wants what is best for us. When we give God full control, He is then free to turn something that seems negative into a blessing.

Tomorrow we will explore how to use open-ended questions in your prayer time.

DAY 2: Using Open-Ended Questions

Fasten your seat belt and prepare to head out on the open road with the Lord. That's what it's like when you learn to start your prayer requests with open-ended questions. You let the Lord pick the route and the final destination. He may take you places in prayer that surprise you!

After beginning your prayer time with thanksgiving and praise, the next step is to ask the Lord, "What's on Your heart?" It's quite common to hear silence, but give the Lord a chance to address something that might not be on your prayer list when you sit down to pray. He might remind you of something you forgot to do, so jot that down. Or He may direct you to pray for someone in need.

If nothing comes to your mind as you listen, then present one of your requests and ask Him what His truth is about that issue. Open-ended questions allow the Lord to show you solutions you might not have considered.

When my daughter believed she had found the right apartment, she wanted me to pray for confirmation. I asked, "Lord, what is Your truth about this apartment?" In my spirit I heard, "Short term." That was it. Just "short term." Neither of us knew what that meant until seven months later. She signed a year-long lease, but before the lease was up, we needed her to move into my mother's house after Mom was transferred to a nursing home. The Lord had given us a heads up about the future even though we did not understand it at the time. That's the beauty of open-ended questions.

At this point, you might be wondering: How does the Lord speak to us? The primary way is through the Scriptures. They are full of wisdom and truth. When you ask God for wisdom, a verse might come to mind that answers your question. Or you might be reading a Scripture that speaks to your spirit.

The Lord has many ways to communicate. He might speak using music or through a dream. A thought or a picture might pop into our minds. It might be through a still, small voice or even circumstances. Sometimes just a nudge. After all, many of our questions do not have answers in God's Word, like where to buy hard-to-find shoes or which college would be best for our son or daughter.

Here is an example. Since I am not music oriented, I pay attention when a tune drifts through my mind. If I am discouraged or need wisdom, when I pray I might hear lyrics that are uplifting or that point me in a certain direction. Many times it is *after* I have prayed and am involved in something else that I hear from the Lord.

Read Matthew 2:13 and 19–20. How did the Lord speak to Joseph?

____

____

____

God protected Jesus by warning Joseph in a dream of Herod's plan to destroy Him. When our minds are asleep, our spirits are still awake, so God can bypass any limits from our logic and reasoning and give us warnings or directives through dreams.

I keep a journal next to my bed as I often ask the Lord to speak to me in a dream. Many dreams disappear quickly, but the ones that linger after I awaken are the ones I record. Most of our dreams are not literal like Joseph's, but they can be symbolic and require seeking the Lord and often a dream dictionary for interpretation (see Recommended Reading in the appendix).

As Christians we can hear three voices: our own, the Lord's, and the enemy's. It's important to silence the voice of our flesh and that of the enemy at the beginning of our prayers like this:

> *I take power and authority over all the power of the enemy. I silence any communication from the kingdom of darkness. I command my flesh to be silent. I choose to receive only from the Holy Spirit, in Jesus' name.*

You may have heard someone say, "I heard God's voice in my spirit" and wondered what that meant. Say a word inside your head—that's how it sounds when the Holy Spirit speaks. It's not an audible voice. It's a quiet voice spoken to your spirit.

Read 1 Kings 19:11–13. How did God speak to Elijah?

____

____

____

Elijah heard the Lord's still, small voice. Since we are made in God's image, we are wired to hear Him as well. One day while I was riding in a friend's car, the engine died. We pulled over to the side of the road. Silently I inquired of the Lord what the problem was and heard "alternator" in my spirit. I asked my friend if that could be the cause but was told it couldn't be. *Oh well,* I thought. *I guess that was just me.* What a surprise to find out the mechanic's diagnosis—a bad alternator.

God wants to communicate with us on a regular basis. I'm sure I have missed His quiet voice numerous times due to rushing around. Hearing the Lord is easier when we stay calm and unhurried and when we expect to hear from Him.

If my son texts me that he's on his way home, I begin to listen for his arrival. Likewise, we need to listen and *expect* the Lord to respond to our prayers even if it's sometime later in the day. Expectation is the key to hearing from the Lord.

Read Genesis 2:15–18. Who initiated the conversation with Adam in the Garden of Eden?

___

___

___

From the beginning of creation, God has been talking to humanity, but many of us have not been taught how to listen. Before realizing that prayer was meant to be a two-way conversation, I simply prayed my list of needs and then solved my problems using my own wisdom. God did not figure directly into the solutions. Now I ask and listen for His wisdom. When dealing with issues that have significant consequences, I ask for confirmations and seek wise counsel.

Many times when God speaks, it's just a nudge or a thought. When the Lord brings a person to mind, I now reach out to them. In the past, I ignored those promptings, not realizing the Holy Spirit was speaking. Before, they were just thoughts to me.

Read John 10:4, 27. Write what Jesus says in verse 27 below.

___

___

___

In Psalm 100:3, who are His sheep?

___

___

___

When we ask Jesus to come into our hearts, His Spirit lives in us. Since we are created in God's image, our spirits are wired to hear Him. Have you ever had thoughts or a knowing in your heart about your circumstances that made you wonder: How did I know that? Write your experience below.

___

___

___

I had been researching flights on the Internet and was about to make my purchase when I felt a hesitancy. It wasn't logical, but I sensed that I should wait and that something would arrive in the mail having to do with the tickets. I had no clue what it would be. Within two days a letter arrived from my mother-in-law, instructing me to use her frequent flyer miles to pay for my ticket. What a pleasant surprise! My impression must have come from the Lord. Remember what John 16:13 (NKJV) says?

> *However, when He, the Spirit of truth, has come, He will guide you into all truth; for He will not speak on His own authority, but whatever He hears He will speak; and He will tell you* ***things to come*** *(emphasis added).*

Knowing about things to come is not a common occurrence but really builds one's faith.

When considering circumstances in relation to prayer, I am cautious about attributing them to the Lord. They can easily be misinterpreted or be a deception from the enemy. For example, right before I began to write a manuscript, I received an unexpected offer to write a medical article. When I prayed about whether to say yes or no, the Lord impressed on my spirit that the article was a distraction from His assignment, so I declined. False opportunities tend to pop up right before the Lord leads in a new direction. The enemy's plan is to misguide us, so we miss God's best.

Not every thought or impression is from the Holy Spirit. First John 4:1 warns us to test the spirits, since the enemy would love to deceive us. We need to ask, "Is this the Lord speaking, the enemy, or my flesh?" We need to be wise in our discernment, and that takes time and practice.

At this point you may be tempted to put these tools right to work the next time you pray; however, I encourage you to wait until the last lesson in week six. Some snares we need to avoid will be discussed in later lessons. In week five we will learn more about how to determine whether we are hearing the Lord or the voice of deception.

By the end of the study, you will have learned about all the pieces to the prayer puzzle and be better able to see the entire picture.

DAY 3: Interceding for Others

"Will you help her?" This question kept popping up in my spirit every few months. Whenever I heard those words, I would see an image in my mind's eye of an acquaintance I'll call Joan. Each time I replied, "Yes, Lord." But after a number of these repetitions, I began to wonder: *Why does He keep asking me this?*

Then came a call from a mutual friend. "Joan's husband died suddenly. Just thought you would want to know." *So that's why the Lord kept asking me.* He had repeated this question five or six times to prepare my heart to obey, knowing it would be a challenge for me.

The Lord knew my heart toward Joan had no resemblance to that of the Good Samaritan. Read Luke 10:25–37. What did the priest and the Levite do when they saw the wounded man?

____

____

____

When the Lord asks us to bear another's burden, sometimes we may feel like passing on the other side of the road. That is how I felt when I received that phone call. How in the world could I help when I barely knew her?

The next day while grocery shopping, I kept hearing *deli tray* in my spirit. My heart was not in tune with God's plan. *I hardly know this woman, Lord.* I wrestled with what I sensed He wanted me to do, but I finally relented and bought an assortment of deli meats and a decorative tray on which to present them.

On returning home I asked the Lord for courage to visit her. Reluctantly, I headed for her house, asking the Lord what to do. *Weep with those who weep* were the words that came into my spirit (see Romans 12:15, NKJV).

As I stepped onto her porch, suddenly I was filled with His compassion. Tears came to my eyes. I spent the next two hours comforting her and praying for her. Read Galatians 6:2 and write the verse below.

____

____

____

God calls us to bear one another's burdens, and that includes praying for others. Read Galatians 5:14 to discover what the law of Christ is and record the verse below.

We are to love our neighbor as ourselves. Sometimes that will stretch us out of our comfort zone. Has that ever happened to you? Jot down your experience below. What made it difficult for you?

Loving our neighbor as ourselves might mean comforting them or assisting them financially or physically, but it also means interceding for them when the Lord puts their names on our hearts. Read Isaiah 53:4–5. This chapter is about Jesus, the Messiah. What does it say that Jesus did for us?

Jesus bore our burdens on the cross. He carried our griefs and sorrows, was beaten for our sins, and gave His life so we could be healed and have eternal life. He was the sacrificial Lamb who removed our sins as far away as the east is from the west (see Psalm 103:12). Christ is the ultimate burden bearer.

In John 17:6–26, we see how Jesus interceded for His disciples and for all who would believe in Him in years to come. This is a perfect example of bearing one another's burdens in prayer.

We are called to do the same for others. Take a moment right now and ask the Lord if there is someone who needs your prayers today. Make note of it here and commit to praying for them.

When the Lord brings someone to mind, find out God's heart for them by asking, "Lord, what do they need?" so you are praying His will for them. Read John 13:34–35 and summarize below.

____

____

____

One of the greatest ways to love others is to pray for them. It can seem like a burden at times, but it brings many rewards. When I left Joan's home, I was so grateful for the opportunity I'd had to comfort her and pray with her.

Loving and praying for our enemies is not something that comes naturally either. It is an act of humility and obedience to the Lord. What does Jesus command us to do in Matthew 5:44?

____

____

____

How did Jesus demonstrate His love for His enemies? Read Luke 23:34 and summarize below.

____

____

____

Take a moment now to ask the Lord if there is anyone you need to forgive. If you are unable to forgive them, ask the Father to soften your heart toward them. This prayer might also help:

> *Lord, I am willing to be made willing to forgive ________. I give You permission to change my heart. Help me see them through Your eyes. In Jesus' name, amen.*

As your heart softens toward this person, make a choice to forgive as an act of your will. Ask the Lord to heal the wounds in your soul that resulted from their behavior and to replace those feelings with love and peace. Then ask the Lord to bless this person and show them His goodness. You may have to repeat this many times until the burden of unforgiveness finally rolls off your back, and you actually feel free of any negative thoughts toward them.

Read Psalm 24:3–4. Summarize the verses below.

One of the ways we prepare our hearts to intercede for ourselves and others is to come before the Lord with a clean heart, which means confessing our sins and forgiving others. We don't want unconfessed sin to hinder the answers to our prayers.

We also want to heed God's direction on how to pray for our enemies so we avoid praying manipulative prayers that reflect unforgiveness or selfish motives.

If we tell someone we are praying for them, we want to be sure we follow up on our commitment. I find it easier to remember to pray for others by writing their names on 3x5 cards. I buy the neon-colored ones to make it fun, and it builds my faith to record the date when those prayers are answered.

We are encouraged not only to bear one another's burdens but also to share our own. I grew up as a loner, very independent. The lack of support from my family forced me to struggle and figure out life on my own. As a result, I did not have any concept of sharing my needs or problems with anyone. In addition, as an extreme introvert, I kept everything to myself. Long into my adult years, I finally learned the importance of sharing needs and concerns with others, giving them an opportunity to stand in the gap for me. I needed both courage and humility to ask for help. As we learned in lesson five last week, prayers of agreement are powerful.

What did Jesus say in Matthew 18:20? Write the verse below.

I love praying with others in person, but we can also "gather together" on a phone call. Distance is not a problem in the spiritual realm.

Is it easy or difficult for you to ask others for prayer? Share your thoughts below. If it is a struggle for you, ask the Lord to help you understand why.

When deciding whether to ask for prayer, pray for discernment. Choose someone who is trustworthy and can keep a confidence if your need is personal. Make it clear whether your concern can be shared with anyone else or whether it is to be kept confidential.

Remember, your prayers matter. Your prayers are powerful. Your prayers will change lives—yours and others.

Have you ever felt completely stumped when you pray, like your prayers are hitting the ceiling and bouncing back? Tomorrow we will discuss seeking wise counsel and fasting.

DAY 4: Fasting and Seeking Wise Counsel

I had slept in on a rare weekday off. My children thought I had gone to work. When I quietly opened my bedroom door, my child's cry shattered my heart.

"I WANT MY MOMMY!" My three-year-old's demand made to my mother, our children's live-in grandmother/caregiver, dismantled my perception of our perfect childcare arrangements. I had the ideal setup, or so I thought up to that moment. This was my first clue that God wanted me to quit my medical practice.

Thoughts of the lawsuit had been consuming me. Every waking moment, I imagined how I would defend myself in a courtroom. I did not need one more thing on my plate, yet I could not ignore my child's plea or the Lord's nudges to quit.

I had a choice: obey or disobey. The decision was the biggest of my professional and family life, and I needed wise counsel. Wise counsel can give us God's perspective when we find ourselves tangled up in knots.

Have you ever faced a situation where nothing made sense, and you didn't know where to turn? Briefly describe your experience below.

____

____

____

What does God promise us in Psalm 32:8?

____

____

____

No matter how hard I prayed, I just could not wrap my head around quitting. My employment provided for the majority of our income. What was God thinking? Where was *His* counsel? Nothing made sense to me.

Proverbs 19:20–21 (NIV) says:

> *Listen to advice and accept discipline, and at the end you will be counted among the wise. Many are the plans in a person's heart, but it is the LORD's purpose that prevails.*

I sure had many plans, but in my heart of hearts, I desperately wanted to be certain of God's plans for me and my family.

Read Proverbs 11:14 (NKJV) and write the verse below.

God's counsel would come through a "multitude of counselors." I sought help from a practice management expert, an attorney, and a physician-attorney. All three led me to the same conclusion. Quit now. Looking back a couple of decades later, it was the best decision I could have made.

God's plan for my family may be vastly different than His plan for yours. You may have to work if you are a single mom. Or the Lord may have called you to full- or part-time employment while you raise your family. I have many friends who laid down their careers to raise their children. We each need to seek God's counsel for our own particular situation. The Lord called me into medicine, and then He called me out in His perfect timing. Read Psalm 37:5 and write the verse below.

I decided to trust the Lord. If I had leaned on my own understanding, human logic and reasoning would have blocked me from obeying the Lord. Sometimes His counsel does not make sense until months or years later. What did Jethro, Moses' father-in-law, instruct Moses to do in Exodus 18:19–26?

Moses ran the risk of exhaustion by being the only one to whom the Israelites came for wise counsel. Jethro advised him to delegate his duties to men of integrity. Moses could handle the larger issues, and the other leaders could judge the smaller matters. That was wise counsel!

If you are struggling with a significant decision, another way to seek God's wisdom is through fasting and prayer. In retrospect, my first experience with fasting as a novice believer is funny. I felt prompted to give up sweets for a certain period. During that time, I attended a group prayer session. At the start of the meeting, the hostess passed around a tempting plate of cookies. My first thought was: *You mean you can pray AND eat cookies!?* No one there seemed to share my unspoken concern as they selected cookies from the plate. Perhaps I was just being tested.

What is the purpose of fasting and prayer? Scripture mentions fasting over seventy times. Perhaps the most famous account is from Esther 4:7–16. Why did Queen Esther fast for three days and nights?

____

____

____

Esther found out about Haman's plot to kill all the Jews. She fasted to find favor with the king and to save the Jews from annihilation.

In another Old Testament account, Ezra led the exiled Jews from Babylon back to Jerusalem to reestablish temple worship. In Ezra 8:21–23, he calls the Jews to fast for what purposes?

____

____

____

Ezra sought God's plan and protection as they returned home. Verse 23 (NIV) says, *He* (God) *answered our prayer.*

You will recall from a previous lesson that Jesus explained to His disciples why He had to leave this earth. Let's look at John 16:12–13 (NKJV) again.

> *I still have many things to say to you, but you cannot bear them now. However, when He, the Spirit of truth, has come, He will guide you into all truth; for He will not speak on His own authority, but whatever He hears He will speak; and He will tell you things to come.*

Since the Day of Pentecost, all believers have been filled with His Spirit upon confessing Jesus Christ as their Lord. Why? So the Lord can continue to speak to His followers. Under the new covenant, Jesus now speaks to us through the Holy Spirit and the Word.

Read Acts 13:2. What happened when a group of believers fasted and prayed in Antioch?

The Holy Spirit directed the believers to send out Saul (Paul) and Barnabas for the Lord's purposes. Fasting and prayer sensitized them to God's Spirit.

Read Daniel 1:3–16 to see how Daniel fasted. Summarize the passage below.

Fasting might involve something as simple as skipping one meal or, like for Daniel, it may consist of limiting what types of food are eaten for a certain period of time. When led to fast, I ask God to show me a specific amount of time to fast and whether to forego certain foods or complete meals. Sometimes my fast does not involve food but rather setting aside extended periods of time to pray.

There are books and online resources you can consult to learn the ins and outs of fasting. If you have a medical condition, check with your physician before attempting to fast.

From the examples in both the Old and New Testaments, fasting is always accompanied by prayer for either guidance, protection, favor, or repentance (see Daniel 9:3, 19). Fasting emphasizes our dependence on God and helps us focus more intently on seeking Him with all our hearts. It heightens our spiritual awareness and sensitivity to the Lord.

Whether we seek the Lord through fasting, wise counsel, or by ourselves, we all want to see our prayers answered. That brings us to John 15:1–10. After reading the passage, write verse 7 below.

What enables our prayers to be answered? Abiding in Christ and having His Word live in our hearts. But what does abiding mean?

Summarize verses 4 and 10 below.

Jesus likened abiding to staying in close fellowship with Him like a branch is vitally connected to a vine. We also need to obey His commandments. Write verse 5 below.

If we want our prayers to bear fruit, we must stay in close relationship with the Lord. As Jesus explains, apart from Him we can do *nothing!* The other fruit that comes from abiding in Christ is mentioned in Galatians 5:22–23. List the fruit we will bear.

The more we spend time in prayer and in the Scriptures, the more Christ-like we become and the more fruit we will bear.

One last thought for today comes from Proverbs 16:3 (AMP):

> *Commit your works to the LORD [submit and trust them to Him],*
> *And your plans will succeed [if you respond to His will and guidance].*

When you pray, ask the Lord to correct you and redirect you. When we release our concerns completely to God, He will cause our thoughts to agree with His. We want to see our situations through God's eyes. Expect to hear from Him, and ask the Holy Spirit to grab your attention during the day if you are distracted and not listening.

Tomorrow we will look at ways to respond when our prayers are answered.

DAY 5: Sharing Your Testimonies

The Statue of Liberty rises majestically from Liberty Island in New York Harbor. Nearby is Ellis Island, where 12 million immigrants arrived from 1892 to 1954 to pursue the American dream. A memorial wall helps us remember the names of many, including my Scottish grandparents who immigrated in the early 1900s.

Remembering God's past blessings builds our faith for future answers to our prayers. Our testimonies of His faithfulness will bless us and others.

Today we have myriad ways to remember God's hand on our lives: diaries, newspaper clippings, photo albums, flash drives, memorabilia, and gifts. A small ceramic angel reminds me of the day I was baptized. Jot down any reminders you have of God's blessings in your life.

____

____

____

As Christ followers, we have the Old and New Testaments to remind us of what God has already done for us through Jesus Christ. As God answered prayer in days of old, He also will answer our prayers, since the Bible assures us God is the same yesterday, today, and forever. What does the Lord say in Malachi 3:6a?

____

____

____

Remember that the same God who parted the Red Sea, defeated the Israelites' enemies, and provided food and water in the wilderness is the same God we serve today. None of your prayer requests go unnoticed by Him.

Commemorating the past is important not only to us, but to the Lord. Before the written Scriptures, the Israelites set up memorials to remind them of their relationship to their God and His supernatural interventions in their lives. Read 1 Samuel 7:10–12. Summarize the verses below.

____

____

____

The Israelites experienced a miraculous victory against the Philistines when the Lord thundered against them, threw them into confusion, and enabled the Israelites to drive them back. Samuel set up a stone to remind them of God's hand of victory. Read Joshua 4:1–8. What did the Lord tell Joshua to do and why?

____

____

____

Look at verse 7. How long did the Lord want the children of Israel to remember this miracle?

____

Why do you think God had them set up a stone memorial? Write your thoughts below.

____

____

____

Read Joshua 4:21–24. Joshua instructed the Israelites how to respond when their children asked, "What are these stones?" What reason is given in verse 24?

____

____

____

Stones were a common way in the Old Testament of remembering God's intervention in the lives of the Hebrews (see Genesis 35:14, Joshua 24:25–27). God didn't want *only* the descendants of Israel to know of His mighty deed, He wanted the people of the *whole earth* to reverence the Lord forever! That certainly foreshadows the spreading of the gospel to all nations.

When our children were in elementary school, I was so impressed by Joshua's stones of remembrance, I bought a decorative glass jar and multicolored polished stones. When a prayer was answered, the child would put a stone in the jar as a reminder of God's goodness to him or her. I made a small journal in which we wrote what the stone stood for. That jar still sits on our kitchen desk as a reminder that God is faithful to answer our prayers.

In our humanity, we tend to forget what God has done for us. Years later, we might even be tempted to take credit ourselves. God warns the Israelites of that tendency in Deuteronomy 8:17–18. Summarize His warning below.

God gave His people a stern warning not to take credit for themselves when they prospered. What did He also warn them about in verses 19–20?

It is important to give God credit where credit is due and to remember His answers to our prayers. Isaiah 42:8 (NKJV) says: *I am the LORD, that is My name; and My glory I will not give to another.*

During trying times when our prayers seem to go unanswered, our faith is strengthened and renewed as we think back and thank God for His goodness to us. If you are currently struggling with what seems to be an unanswered prayer, what has God done for you in the past that you could thank Him for today while you wait?

God also established the Jewish feasts as another way for His people to remember His miraculous interventions in their lives. As Christians, we have several parallel celebrations that the Jewish feasts foreshadowed, one of which is Passover.

Read Exodus 12:1–14. The Passover feast commemorated the Exodus from Egypt and enslavement. Summarize verses 13–14 below.

The Jews were instructed to apply the blood of a spotless lamb over their doorposts so that the angel of death would not harm anyone in that household. Only the first-born of the Egyptians would perish.

Passover foreshadowed the crucifixion. Christ's blood, shed for us, frees us from the slavery of sin and guarantees eternal life. Like the Passover lamb, not one of Jesus' bones was broken. Our yearly celebration on Resurrection Sunday or Easter reminds us to thank and honor Jesus, whose sacrifice paid for our salvation and whose resurrection is the very foundation of our faith.

In addition to remembering what God has done in the past, we also need to be sensitive to what God is doing in our lives right now. Our busy lifestyles make it easy to miss God's fingerprints. Keeping a gratitude journal is one way to record how God is working in our lives daily. Thanking the Lord when we see His blessings also makes us more aware of His presence. According to James 1:17, where does every good gift come from?

____

____

____

We can teach ourselves to thank the Lord for even the smallest of blessings: no line at the post office, a front row parking space, or perhaps someone let me go first in line or made room for me to switch lanes in snarled traffic. After I load my groceries in the car or fill up my gas tank, I take time to thank Him for His provision. When we thank and honor the Lord for every blessing, He multiplies them back to us.

Read John 4:28–29, 39. This is the story of the woman at the well. After her encounter with Jesus, where does the woman go and what does she do? What effect did her testimony have on other Samaritans in her city?

____

____

____

Read Luke 8:26–39. What did Jesus tell the man who was set free from demons to do?

____

____

____

In Mark 5:19 (NKJV), Jesus told the man to share his experience with his friends as well. Do you find it easy or difficult to share with others what God has done in your life? Please explain.

Sharing our answered prayers can build the faith of those around us. Be sensitive to the Spirit's leading. If you're uncertain about what to share, ask the Lord to block from your mind the topics He doesn't want you to discuss. Some people will not be receptive, but others will be blessed when you share.

My friends know I will pray about almost anything. God created the universe, and He also created subatomic particles, yet some Christians believe we should only pray about big-ticket items like where to live or work. However, the Scriptures do not limit what we can seek God for. The Contemporary English Version (CEV) of 1 Peter 5:7 says this: *God cares for you, so turn all your worries over to him.* All means *all.*

Having said that, we need to be mindful not to view God as a supernatural Santa. If you are a parent, though, doesn't it delight you to meet your child's needs? God is our loving heavenly Father who delights to give good gifts to us, His children.

The Scriptures say that we do not have because we do not ask, or we ask with wrong motives. As a friend once told me, when we solve our problems without God, we are the ones who get the credit. But when we pray and seek God's wisdom and assistance, then He gets the glory, and our faith and trust in Him increases.

God is available to us any time, any day through the Holy Spirit who dwells within us. You matter to Him, and Your needs matter to Him. He is never too busy or too far away to hear your prayers.

My walk with the Lord has taught me that nothing is too small or too big to pray about. I will share some of my testimonies with you next week as we discuss how to pray for family and friends.

WEEK FOUR

DAY 1: Prayers for Salvation of Family and Friends

"When I die, I know I am going to heaven, and I want you to be there," I pleaded.

"I don't believe in that. When you die, you die. That's it," she responded with finality.

My heart grieved to hear the coldness in my mother's voice.

Perhaps the most painful part of life as a Christian is to have family members—especially parents, a spouse, or our children—reject Jesus as Lord and Savior. One of my first prayer requests when I got saved was for my mother's salvation. She had become a single mom when I was a teenager. The divorce caused her to become angry at God, and she stopped attending church. Whenever I tried to share my faith, she responded angrily or indifferently.

Praying for the salvation of family and friends can sometimes make us feel helpless. Why won't they listen to the Good News? Why don't they care about what matters most to us?

After many years of praying, the Lord showed me in a dream that I would not be the one to lead my mother to Christ. He assured me: "I will have the last dance with her." How was God going to do that when none of her friends were committed Christians? It made no sense, but at least I had hope that someone would cross her path and share the gospel with her.

Are you praying for someone who does not know Jesus? Write his or her name here.

____

I prayed many prayers for my mother over the years, but my simplest one sounded like this: "Lord, don't let her die unsaved." God kept His promise to me just months before she went to be with Him.

I knew that praying for my mother to accept Christ was God's will. Were there times that I wondered if it would ever happen? Yes, but that did not stop me from praying. We are to pray without ceasing and leave the results up to Him.

We must be *convinced* of the truth that God does not want anyone to die unsaved (2 Peter 3:9). Otherwise, we run the risk of giving up and not persevering in prayer.

We know that we are praying His will for that unsaved person when we pray for their salvation.

Jesus declares in Matthew 18:11–14 that He came to save the lost. Summarize verse 12 below.

____

____

____

Be assured, your lost loved one is being sought after by Jesus Christ, our heavenly Shepherd.

We learned earlier that God assures us, if we ask anything according to His will, He hears us, and that we have what we ask (1 John 5:14–15).

Our prayers are vitally important, but ultimately it is the Holy Spirit who draws a person to Christ (see John 16:7–11). What does Jesus say in John 6:44 about how a person comes to know Him?

____

____

____

We see that only the Father can draw a person to Christ through the conviction of the Holy Spirit. We share our beliefs, but we leave the results to the Lord.

Why aren't some people saved? They might have grown up attending church, had godly parents who loved them and prayed for their souls, yet they never asked Jesus to be their Lord, or they walked away from what they were taught. Studies show that 70 percent of children from Christian families abandon their Christian roots when they graduate from high school. That's an astounding statistic! Thankfully, many return to the Lord as they mature.

We can understand why some people reject God by reading 2 Corinthians 4:4. Summarize that verse below.

____

____

____

The enemy of our souls, the devil, wants to take as many people as he can to hell. Satan's goal is to steal a person's God-given destiny and destroy any possibility of a relationship with God. He is a thief and the father of lies, according to John 8:44.

Read Romans 1:18–24. Summarize verse 19 below.

____

____

____

Verse 19 tells us that God has shown Himself to all people. Verse 20 explains how. Write that verse in your own words.

____

____

____

Anyone who looks at what God has created can't help but see His handprints on the world. However, because of free will, many choose not to put their trust in Him. When God challenged me to choose Him, my first thought was not to choose. I wanted complete control of my life.

As someone once said, we all have a god. If it's not the Creator, it is something else: self, money, power, or other things we desire.

Verse 21 explains what happens to a person when they do not acknowledge Him as God. Summarize those reasons below.

____

____

____

I can look back and see how my heart was darkened all those years when I lived for myself and not God. I believed the enemy's lies, not God's truth. What does Jeremiah 17:9 say about man's heart?

____

____

____

Ouch—wicked and deceitful! When someone is deceived, they are not aware of the deception. It's part of our fallen nature, or original sin. Keep that in mind when praying for those who do not acknowledge Jesus Christ as their Lord. They may be involved in offensive or self-destructive behaviors, but if we focus on their behavior, we may lose sight of our main goal, which is to love and pray for them.

One afternoon I was seeing patients in the dermatology clinic. A family practice resident (doctor in training) was following me around to learn about skin diseases. After a few days he asked me, "Are you a Christian?"

"Yes. Why do you ask?" His question puzzled me.

"I thought so. It's the way you treat your patients. I thought you must be a Christian."

His comment was very convicting. I had not given one thought to how my behavior might influence someone else in their view toward Christianity until that moment. Our actions do speak louder than our words. How are we reflecting Christ to others?

Take a moment to reflect. Is your unsaved loved one seeing Christ in you? Is there something you would like to change?

____

____

____

None of us is perfect. We must not let past mistakes keep us from sharing our love of Christ with others. God can even use our faults because as we mature in our Christian walk, those close to us will see us change and become more Christ-like. They will see the difference He makes in our lives. That is the power of our personal testimony.

Scripture gives us a heads up on the times we live in. Read 2 Timothy 3:2.

How does Paul describe the people in the "last days"?

____

____

____

Do you see any evidence in our culture that mirrors what Paul said? Record your observations below.

____

____

____

Even as Christians, we can be self-centered at times. Those who do not believe may be even more self-centered. If we understand what goes on in the minds of those unbelieving family members and friends, we can pray with more compassion. In 2 Timothy 4:3–4 we are given more insight into the unbeliever's mind. Summarize the passage below.

The Amplified translation (AMP) says that they will *wander off into myths and man-made fictions*. We are seeing that today with so-called Christians who deny original sin, the need for Christ's atonement, and believe many other manmade fictions that contradict Scripture.

Years ago I was particularly upset about someone I cared for who had accepted Christ and then fell away rather quickly. To console me, another friend reminded me of the parable of the sower.

Read that parable in Matthew 13:3–8 and the explanation in Matthew 13:18–23. Even though someone might hear the good news of Jesus Christ, what can happen to the truth that they have heard?

This parable helped me to understand what had happened, although it did not make it any less painful. People make choices, some of which are not wise.

We also need to have a firm foundation for our faith so that we can share it with unbelievers. Some have bought into the lie that there are many ways to heaven. However, what does 1 Timothy 2:5 say? Summarize the verse below.

This verse clearly states there is only one God and one mediator between God and people—Jesus Christ. That excludes Allah, Buddha, and any others that might claim to have a path to heaven.

Acts 4:12 backs that up with a little more emphasis. Write the verse below.

> ____
> ____
> ____

"No other name" means salvation is entirely through faith in Jesus Christ. Period.

In my prayer time, I find it boosts my spirits to personalize and declare Job 22:30 (AMP) like this: "You will even rescue the one for whom I intercede who is not innocent." Then I list the names of those for whose salvation I am interceding.

I also declare Job 42:2 (AMP): *I know that You can do all things, and that no thought or purpose of Yours can be restrained.* I know God wants these friends and loved ones to be saved, and these verses help me persevere in praying for their souls.

If the person you are praying for has offended you or mistreated you, praying with forgiveness in your heart is vital. That may mean that every time you come to the Lord to pray for them, you forgive again...and again. Forgiving them does not excuse their mistreatment; it frees you to pray for and treat them with love.

Remind yourself that they are deceived and are unable to act in a godly manner because their hearts and thoughts are darkened. Ask God to bless them and show them His goodness and love. Ask the Holy Spirit to show you ways to demonstrate Christ's love to them.

We have an assurance that God will keep His promises to us in Jeremiah 1:12 (AMP): *I am [actively] watching over My word to fulfill it.* By declaring Scripture over our loved ones, we know He is watching over those promises to fulfill them.

Here are some suggested prayers you can pray for your lost loved ones.

Lord, I lift up __________ to You and ask that You would:

- *Soften their heart to receive Your truth.*
- *Give them a teachable mind and heart.*
- *Give them eyes to see and ears to hear the good news of Jesus Christ.*
- *Send the right person to share Jesus with them.*

Tomorrow we will talk about prayers for protection and health.

DAY 2: Prayers for Health

"I can only stay a short time. I'm not feeling well."

I welcomed my friend in, disappointed that our time would be cut short by her queasy stomach, which began when she woke up and had not abated. She almost canceled our visit.

I stretched forth my hand toward her and prayed. "Lord, let Your presence rest upon her and release Your healing power into her digestive system. Cause it to function as You originally intended it to. Take away any queasiness and restore her health, in Jesus' name."

Three hours later she got up from the table, having enjoyed the shortbread, chocolate, and tea without a hint of symptoms. "I feel fine!" she exclaimed.

Today's topic is prayer for healing, which can be a controversial subject within the body of Christ. Some believe that all miracles and healing ceased when the last apostle died or the Scriptures were written. That is their experience. However, I have experienced and seen so many healings that to deny God heals today would be to say God is not the same yesterday, today, and forever (see Malachi 3:6 and Hebrews 13:8).

Read Matthew 7:7–11. Summarize verse 11 below in your own words.

____

____

____

Jesus makes it clear that He wants us to ask for good gifts. What parent would not want to give good gifts to their child? Does that mean that every time I pray for healing it appears instantly? No. In fact, most of the time, my own healings have come over a period of time. Some have yet to appear even though I have sought the Lord for years and years about them.

I remember listening to a pastor tell the congregation, "I have the answer to why some people are not healed." He paused to create anticipation, then continued. "The answer is, I don't know." He had seen hundreds, perhaps thousands of healings during his mission trips around the world, yet many others were not healed. Why? First Corinthians 13:9 (NIV) says that *we know in part*. We don't always understand why some prayers for healing are not answered in the affirmative, but we would miss many good gifts if we failed to pray at all. My default is always to pray and leave the results up to the Lord.

Read Psalm 105:37. This verse is talking about the exodus from Egypt. Crossing the desert wilderness to reach the Promised Land would put a strain on anyone, especially for the elderly. But what does this verse tell us?

God must have healed all who left Egypt if there was not one feeble person among them.

Read Matthew 4:23–24. Jesus traveled about Galilee, preaching in synagogues and teaching. What else did He do that brought crowds?

Jesus developed such a reputation for healing and deliverance that verse 24 says His fame even spread to Syria. That's without social media, cell phones, and the Internet!

There are some things we can be certain of about healing.

Read Mark 1:40–42. What did the leper ask Jesus to do?

The leper was not sure if Jesus would heal him, so he asked if Jesus was *willing*. How did Jesus respond?

Jesus affirmed that He was willing to heal the leper. He reached out and touched him, and the leper was healed. Since Jesus is the same today as He was back then, we know He is willing to heal us too.

Read Matthew 9:20–22 and summarize below.

In verse 22, what reason does Jesus give for why she was healed?

Jesus attributed the woman's healing to her faith in Him. Reading along further in Matthew 9, we see in verses 27–30 that two blind men received their sight. What did Jesus say to them in verse 29?

Again, we are told that faith was the key factor in Jesus' willingness to heal someone. In an earlier lesson, we learned that Jesus could do few miracles in His hometown because of a lack of faith, or unbelief in Him. Fortunately, it only takes a mustard-seed amount of faith for our prayers to be answered.

A careful reading of the gospels shows us that Jesus *never* inflicted disease or sickness on anyone as a judgment or punishment. In fact, He healed everyone who came to Him.

Read the commission that Jesus gave to the eleven disciples right before He ascended to heaven in Mark 16:15–18. In verse 18 He mentions the laying on of hands. For what purpose?

Did Jesus limit laying hands on the sick to just the eleven or to those who believe?

Jesus instructed them to preach the gospel and baptize those who accept Christ. Then He declared that these signs will follow *those who believe* (v. 17). That includes you and me. There aren't any qualifiers or disqualifiers.

Read Acts 3:1–10 and summarize what happened below.

What is amazing is that the Scripture does not say that the man asked to be healed. He was expecting to receive a handout but received something far better!

What does it say about healing in Mark 6:13 when Jesus sent the disciples out to preach in various towns and cities?

What are James' instructions to the Church in James 5:14?

The oil was a means of consecrating the person being prayed for and represents the Holy Spirit. It did not have a medicinal purpose. Verse 15 (NKJV) says that *the prayer of faith will save the sick*. James' instructions hold true for the Church today.

Read John 14:12 and write the verse below.

Again, Jesus does not limit His instructions to just His disciples. *Whoever believes in me* means anyone who believes in Jesus Christ is authorized to do the same things He did and even greater works. Since much of His ministry involved healing and deliverance, we are to go and do likewise.

In James 1:22, James urges us to be doers of the word, not just hearers. As followers of Christ, we are encouraged to pray for healing. If we don't believe God still heals today, we won't pray. If we don't pray, we won't see healings. Unfortunately, it's self-reinforcing. Why not step out in faith, take a risk, and start praying? James 1:25 (NIV) says that those who do the works *will be blessed in what they do.*

Read Luke 4:16–21. Jesus visited His hometown of Nazareth and read from the book of Isaiah. He declared in verse 21 that He is the fulfillment of those verses. List several things that He is anointed to do, mentioned in verse 18.

We learn from that passage that Jesus was sent to heal both physically and emotionally. Summarize Matthew 8:17 below.

Jesus fulfilled the prophecy from Isaiah 53:4 that says He bore our griefs and sorrows, which includes physical and spiritual sicknesses in the original language of the Scriptures.

Read Matthew 9:2–7. What clue do we have as to why some are sick or infirm?

Jesus demonstrated that unconfessed sin may be an issue that needs to be dealt with before healing occurs (see also John 5:14).

Read John 9:1–3. Was sin the reason the man was born blind? Summarize those verses below.

Jesus makes it clear that not every disease or infirmity is due to personal or generational sins. Regardless of the underlying cause, Jesus was always willing to heal during His time on earth.

A mystery remains as to why some people are not healed, but I never fail to pray for healing for myself and others. My prayer might sound like this:

> *Lord, I ask for Your presence and healing power to come upon (name of person). Release Your glory on their body. Heal their (body part). I command any sickness or disease to leave their body. In Jesus' name.*

If symptoms are urgent or indicate an emergency, I will pray while seeking traditional medical intervention. If there is any improvement at all while praying, I will repeat the prayer and ask for more of God's healing power until all symptoms are gone. If nothing more happens, I will ask the Lord if there is anything blocking the healing and address that in prayer.

Here are some Scriptures that I have personalized and declare out loud over myself when I pray for healing. You can insert someone's name and personalize these paraphrased verses for them as well.

- Your words are life to those who find them and health to all my flesh (based on Proverbs 4:20–22).
- You sent forth Your word and healed me and delivered me from destruction (based on Psalm 107:20).
- Jesus bore my sins in His body on the cross that I, having died to sin, might live for righteousness, and by His wounds I have been healed (based on 1 Peter 2:24).
- Jesus was wounded for my transgressions. He was bruised for my iniquities. The chastisement for my peace was upon Him, and by His stripes I am healed (based on Isaiah 53:5).

DAY 3: Prayers for Employment, Finances, and Stewardship

Making wise decisions depends on how much we rely on God's Spirit of truth and wisdom. He is all knowing, so whose wisdom, His or yours, would you prefer to rely on, especially when it comes to finances, employment, and stewardship?

Learning to listen to God and obeying His guidance is far more efficient than undoing poor choices. Relying on logic and reasoning is not a sin, but submitting your reasoning to God's will is vastly superior to depending on human thinking alone.

Ask, listen, confirm, and obey are the prayer principles I depend on. Frugality has been a byword for most of my life. When I became a stay-at-home mom, living within our means became even more important. I needed to make the wisest choices about spending less money.

Before I learned that prayer involves listening to God, I simply recited my list of needs and ended the prayer. I relied *solely* on my logic and reasoning to make decisions.

Here's an example. I wanted to buy a Christmas gift for a friend. My monologue prayer sounded something like this: "Lord, I need a Christmas gift for Barbara. Please give me wisdom about what to buy her. In Jesus' name, amen." Then I would go shopping, perhaps for hours, or days, wondering what to buy. I might make several purchases and fret about whether she would like them. Although there is nothing inherently wrong with praying like this, I would like to propose a more efficient way to pray.

After learning to pray *and* listen, this is how my prayer actually sounded: "Lord, I need to find a Christmas gift for Barbara. I have no idea what to get her, but I know You do. Please show me what she would like."

Here's where the difference comes in. After praying, I sat and listened, waiting for the Lord to respond. I had an impression of a fleece jacket, but this was right after fleece came on the market. It only came in vests, so I reminded God of that fact. I listened again: *Fleece jacket*. That's all that came to mind. To test it out, I asked where I would find such a jacket (if it really did exist!). A store in a part of town I do not usually frequent came to mind. To test this out, I drove to the store. There on a clearance rack was a periwinkle fleece jacket on sale. I was stunned. My friend loved the gift. One trip to the right store to buy the right gift at the right price. By listening, I received a personalized answer to prayer that saved me time, money, and frustration.

Praying and *listening* is like going on a spiritual treasure hunt. What a faith-builder!

Read Proverbs 3:13–14 and write the verses below.

God's wisdom far exceeds our limited wisdom; it's even better than silver and gold. How does the Apostle Paul describe the world's wisdom in 1 Corinthians 1:19?

We have access to God's wisdom every day. Why pass that up when it comes to any of our decisions? What does Proverbs 8:11 say about the Lord's wisdom?

All the things we could possibly desire cannot compare with the Lord's wisdom, and it's ours simply for the asking!

Proverbs 9:10 tells us the fear of the Lord is the beginning of wisdom. Learning to rely on His guidance is a game changer for financial decisions.

Read John 21:1–11. Seven of Jesus' disciples fished all night and caught nothing. What happened when Jesus intervened with His wisdom?

These experienced fishermen failed to catch any fish until Jesus told them to cast their net on the right side of the boat. Is it logical that there were no fish on the left side but 153 on the right? The Lord's wisdom may not make sense at first, but obeying His direction brings abundant provision.

When it comes to employment, we need to be careful about whether God is directing our choice, or whether we are deciding solely based on salary. Have we asked whether He wants us to work or stay at home? Have we asked where He wants us to work and whether it should be full- or part-time? God has specific plans for our lives. We don't want to miss His best for ourselves and our families.

Jesus warns us about the danger of having wrong priorities. What did He say in Matthew 6:24?

___

___

___

Without even realizing it, we can become slaves to money. We must guard our hearts and make a conscious decision that money will not control us. This is demonstrated in the story of the rich young ruler who chose money instead of following Jesus (see Matthew 19:16–22). What does 1 Timothy 6:10 warn us about money?

___

___

___

If making a lot of money, rather than obeying the Lord, is our sole focus, the Bible warns that money could lead us astray from our faith and cause sorrow. What if the Lord has assignments for you at a job with less pay? Or as a volunteer in a ministry?

If conditions at your job begin to sour, it may be tempting to quit. Pray about whether the Lord would have you stay or look for other employment. One of my friends sought the Lord's will when his company began making an ungodly product. On the surface it might seem logical to quit, but he was directed to stay for a period of time in order to speak God's truth to the leadership there.

When we are sincere about obeying only His will for our lives and when we ask for His guidance, God will provide.

What did the Lord do for the Israelites during their wilderness wandering according to Deuteronomy 29:5?

___

___

___

What about praying over your home and your possessions? God can make them last much longer than you expect. The last time I took my nine-year-old car in for service,

I prayed that the Lord would make it like new so it would not need any repairs. I was stunned to hear the mechanic say several times, "It's like it's brand new." Prayer can be a huge money saver! What does Isaiah 30:21 assure us when we pray?

___

___

___

When you honor the Lord with your finances, He will guide and direct your choices. Seek His wisdom for investing and spending. It pays off in the long run.

Before entering an electronics store to purchase a digital camera, I prayed with a friend concerning which brand to buy. I knew which camera was rated number one by Consumer Reports, but I wanted God's wisdom. He directed me toward a different camera. I found out later that another friend had purchased the brand recommended by Consumer Reports and did not like it. She preferred the one I bought. It paid to pray.

When I needed to replace my sixteen-year-old car, I could not find any dealership with the model and color I wanted. In fact, a salesman told me he had bought up all those end-of-the-year models and that such a car did not exist in our area. So I continued to pray. I felt directed to look online again, even though my previous searches had been fruitless.

This time I located the exact car and color. Plus, the dealer was offering a sizeable discount. Then I asked the Lord what to offer for the car. I saw a picture of a person in a very tight space and heard in my spirit, "No wiggle room."

After taking a test drive, I sat down with a salesperson and made an offer. His manager responded, "This is already our lowest price. There's no wiggle room." What a confirmation that it was a fair price!

Another way to be sure we are in God's will concerning finances is in the stewardship of our money. What promises does the Lord make in Malachi 3:10 about tithing?

___

___

___

Jesus affirmed tithing in Matthew 23:23, although this concept is not taught in all churches. However, according to Luke 6:38, even giving generously will bless us in return.

Summarize that verse below.

Our giving will be multiplied back to us. That is a win-win prospect. This truth is also confirmed in 2 Corinthians 9:6–7. Summarize those verses below.

We have all heard the phrase, you reap what you sow. This applies in all aspects of our lives including finances.

Verse 7 instructs us to give cheerfully. I learned that the hard way on one of my shopping trips. As I approached the grocery store, I heard the Salvation Army bell and saw the red kettle in the lobby. Not wanting to be embarrassed by not giving, but also not feeling at all generous that day, I determined to give a few dollars when I left the store. When I exited the store, the kettle was gone; the volunteer was on break. It was clear in my heart that God loves a cheerful giver, and I was not one at the time. I repented for my wrong motives and asked Him to change my heart. On my next trip to the store, I gave cheerfully, not begrudgingly.

I grew up with a poverty mentality due to our financial straits. But I have since learned that the Lord takes delight in the prosperity of His children (Psalm 35:27).

What does the Apostle John pray in 3 John 2? Write the verse below.

The Lord wants us to prosper in all things. One reason for prosperity is seen in Luke 10:30–37. Briefly summarize below.

How can we be good Samaritans if we do not have extra to give to those in need? Regarding the kindness of the good Samaritan, Jesus tells us in verse 37, "Go and do likewise."

Prosperity is not to be an end in itself. Wealth is not for hoarding, but for doing the will of God, to bless others in need, and to leave an inheritance for our children (see Proverbs 13:22).

Here are some prayers and declarations regarding finances:

- *Lord, please multiply our finances and give me wisdom to steward them.*
- *Lord, grant me a cheerful and generous heart to give as You direct.*
- *I am blessed to be a blessing.*
- *I am prospering and being in good health just as my soul prospers.*

DAY 4: Prayers for Time Management

Does God care about the choices we make? The everyday small choices that may not seem like such a big deal?

I learned that the answer is a resounding yes! One of the mothers in my MOPS (Mothers of Preschoolers) group needed childcare so she could take her son for daily chemotherapy. She asked for volunteers and needed to know by Friday. I sought the Lord, pressured by my own feelings that I should step up even though childcare was my least favorite thing to do. By Friday I was exasperated. "Lord, if You don't show me what You want me to do, I am going to sign up." I sat rocking in my chair frustrated that He had not indicated His will. Very clearly, I then heard in my spirit, *I did not call you to do childcare.*

Instead of being relieved, I then struggled with pride. What would the other mothers think of my not volunteering? However, the firm conviction that I would be out of God's will if I signed up won out. It was a watershed moment that God does care about how I spend my time and what I volunteer for. I also learned that "shoulds," guilt, and pride are not to determine my decisions.

Two weeks later the same mother needed some volunteers to learn a medical procedure in case she needed backup for her son. My spirit leaped in excitement. That was right up my medical alley. I had peace and felt enthusiasm about signing up. If I had committed to the childcare, I would not have been available to help her medically.

David wrote these startling words about his life in the womb in Psalm 139:16 (AMP):

> *Your eyes have seen my unformed substance:*
> *And in Your book were all written*
> *The days that were appointed for me,*
> *When as yet there was not one of them [even taking shape].*

It sure sounds like God planned certain tasks before we were even born. That doesn't mean I am wondering every minute of the day, *What does God want me to do now?* I cover that base each morning by asking the Holy Spirit to take charge over my time, then I try to stay tuned in to His leading if He wants to redirect me as the day progresses.

We have free will and freedom to write what is necessary for ourselves and our family on the calendar. However, when it comes to committing my time to volunteer or to work, I do seek the Lord's will specifically.

What does Ecclesiastes 3:1 say about time?

____

____

____

There are two words for "time" in Greek, *chronos* and *kairos*. The first means chronological time, referring to the time on the clock or calendar. The second means an opportune time, God's time for something He specifically wants done. If I had committed to childcare, I would have missed the Lord's *kairos* time, His favorable time that He planned for me to help out medically.

My heart's desire is to be at the right place at the right time, *His* time. I don't want to miss when He interrupts me, like the example I gave earlier about assisting the lady who fell in the grocery store.

What does Ephesians 5:15–16 say about time? Summarize in your own words below.

____

____

____

Redeeming the time means we are to make the best use of our time. Most, if not all of us, probably wish we could pack 48 hours into a 24-hour day; we have more on our to-do lists than we can possibly manage.

However, if we are not mindful of committing our time to the Lord each day, we run the risk of having little time at all for Him, or of being so harried that we fail to realize when He is trying to get our attention. We don't want to miss those *kairos* times because they build our faith and trust in Him.

Most days I feel somewhat like a hermit crab, content to stay in my shell. My natural inclination is to decline requests for my time unless the Lord directs me to accept. My home is my comfort zone where I renew my energy, but I have learned the importance of praying about opportunities so as not to miss divine appointments.

Conversely, if you are a social butterfly, your calendar may be so jammed with commitments that you run the risk of missing some of God's invitations. Both homebodies and socializers do well to commit their time to the Lord for His divine alignments and assignments. Read Ephesians 2:10 and write the verse below.

____

____

____

You were born at this period in time for specific assignments for which God equipped you. Some of those assignments may seem impossible or uncomfortable. However, what does Philippians 4:13 tell us? Write the verse below.

Many of the assignments God directs me to do are outside my comfort zone or natural abilities. For that very reason, I am forced to draw on God's strength. I become acutely aware that apart from Him I can do nothing (see John 15:5). None of us likes to feel weak or unfit for a task, but that is what drives us toward a deeper relationship with God. That is what builds our faith, trust, and dependence in Him. Whatever He calls us to do, He will equip us to do (see Philippians 4:19). We are assured in Philippians 1:6 that when God begins a good work in us, He will complete it.

How did Jesus describe us in Matthew 5:13–16, and what was His concern?

Part of displaying a good testimony for Jesus is how we behave around others. Jesus teaches that we are to be salt and light, which means reflecting Christ's character to those around us. Is there a way to incorporate His character even in mundane things like shopping?

Writing "help someone" on my grocery list reminds me to be salt and light and alert to the needs of other shoppers. I have had the joy of assisting an elderly woman retrieve an item on a top shelf, directing a woman in a motorized cart to the correct aisle for what she needed, and praying for people with medical issues.

What about our free time? Does it matter what we choose for entertainment?

Remember what the Word of God says in 1 Corinthians 3:16? Our bodies are a temple of God, and His Spirit lives in each one of us.

God is not a party pooper as some of us were raised to think. Jesus asked the Father to give us His joy, but He also prayed that God would sanctify us with His truth. His Word is truth (see John 17:13, 17). To sanctify means to set apart. Being mindful that God's Holy Spirit lives in each of us, are we choosing entertainment that pleases or grieves His Spirit?

How does Ephesians 5:1 instruct us to live our lives?

God is a holy God, and we are to imitate Him not just at work or church but daily. The Apostle Peter makes that clear in 1 Peter 1:15–16. Write the verses below.

What we see and hear affects our hearts and minds. We taught our kids to guard their eyes. I instructed them to leave any class in which the teacher was showing movies that they were not comfortable viewing—those with violence or sexuality. On more than one occasion, one of my children asked to be excused and sat out in the hallway while the class watched a video. By setting high standards as our children grow up, they will more easily recognize inappropriate choices when they are out of the nest. What does John 16:7–8 say the Holy Spirit will convict the world of?

One of the ways we mature in Christ is to respond to the Spirit's conviction of sin and righteousness. That means being sensitive to any hesitation you may feel about something that is not pleasing to the Lord. Remember that Jesus sees whatever you watch. Guard your heart and soul and those of your family.

For a partial list of things to avoid, read Ephesians 5:2–7. Verse 8 tells us that we were once darkness, but now we are to walk as children of the light. Summarize verses 10–11 below.

God's Word urges us not to associate with darkness, or sin. We are to be in the world but not of it (see John 17:16–17). A good question to ask is: How will this affect my soul (or my child's soul)? (See Matthew 6:22-23.) Ask the Holy Spirit to give you discernment to make wise choices that please the Lord. Read 1 Thessalonians 4:1–8 and summarize what the Apostle Paul wrote in verse 7.

____

____

____

We are called to holiness in all aspects of our lives. Satan uses entertainment, especially television, movies, and the Internet, as a major temptation to sin. When faced with choices, use Scripture as your guide. It is helpful to ask yourself: Is God's Spirit the *Holy* Spirit or the happy and entertained spirit?

First Thessalonians 4:8 says that when we reject holiness, we are not rejecting other people, but God. In this culture where even young children have access to the Internet, we must be vigilant to set safeguards on what their eyes see and what enters their hearts.

I gave our children permission to call me at any time, day or night, if they found themselves in an uncomfortable or offensive situation. Only on one occasion did I have to go pick one of them up at midnight. They knew our standards, and I prayed that they would have the courage of their convictions to say no to their peers. I gave them permission to put the blame on me if they needed to extricate themselves from inappropriate behavior on the part of their friends.

Here are some prayers and declarations for you and your family:

- *Lord, sensitize me to what offends You.*
- *Put a check in my spirit if something is unclean.*
- *Help me be in the right place at the right time and to recognize where You are at work.*
- *Teach me to use my time wisely to honor You.*

DAY 5: Prayers for Church, Community, and Country

I was just about to drop off my son at school when he elbowed me firmly. *What?* He'd never done that before. He exited the car without a word. We had just heard an announcement on the Christian radio station about a rally that day at our state capital regarding a proposed Heartbeat Bill to curb abortion. Me? Get involved in politics? Never. At least that was how I used to feel.

All the way home I could not stop thinking of what I just heard and what my son had done. *Do you want me to drive up there, Lord?* No answer, but the thought would not leave me. I had just enough time to pack a lunch and start driving if I were to make the meeting.

Perhaps you have experienced similar feelings. *Politics is just not my thing,* you've thought. Praying for the church, community, and national issues was never on my prayer list—until that nudge.

Ever since that experience, I have been convicted that all believers need to include prayers for the nation, especially now that Christian values and beliefs have been sidelined in all areas of our culture, including schools, media, government, and sadly, even some churches.

Timothy oversaw the church in Ephesus. The Apostle Paul wrote him a letter instructing him on how to handle problems and leadership in the church. What did Paul instruct Timothy and the church to do in 1 Timothy 2:1–3?

____

____

____

We know from Genesis 1:28 that God has given people the responsibility to steward the earth. Those in authority need our prayers for wisdom.

In Matthew 6:10, Jesus taught His disciples to pray for God's kingdom to come, His will to be done on earth as it is in heaven. Our prayers and declarations of Scripture play a part in bringing the culture of heaven to earth. We are to pray that God's will be made known to those in leadership and made manifest in our nation. Read Psalm 33:12 and write the verse below.

____

____

____

To have a godly nation, we need godly leaders and righteous laws. When God is honored, the nation is blessed.

Read 2 Chronicles 7:14. God instructed Solomon that if the nation strayed into sin, the people had a remedy for removing God's judgment and healing the land. Describe that remedy below.

God was giving Israel a heads up. If they were to fall into such sinfulness that the entire nation deserved judgment, God would relent and bless them when they humbled themselves and repented. His holiness requires judgment, but His unconditional love brings restoration. Read Isaiah 5:20 and write the verse below.

When I pray for our nation, I ask the Lord to remove from leadership those who call evil good and good evil, and to replace them with godly men and women who are patriots. I also pray for the fear of the Lord to be on those in leadership, for holiness to sweep over our country, and for revival to spread over every nation. We need leaders who have the courage to stand for what is right in God's sight.

In Matthew 10:26 (NIV), Jesus says that there is nothing concealed that will not be disclosed, or hidden that will not be made known. What does Proverbs 14:34 say?

Since righteousness exalts a nation, what hidden sins do you think the Lord would want to be revealed and dealt with in a nation?

One of my frequent prayers for our country is that the Lord will deal with corruption, treason, and fraud, and that He will overturn all unrighteous laws. How do we know that is His will? Read Psalm 89:14. What does it say about God's throne?

God is a holy, righteous judge of the nations. A Scripture that I declare daily is Psalm 103:6 (NKJV), which says God *executes righteousness and justice for all who are oppressed*. As we intercede, we can ask the Lord to raise up godly judges, governors, senators, and representatives to promote His kingdom on earth.

We can pray similar prayers for the leadership of our communities—for righteous mayors, city council members, school board members, teachers, law enforcement officers, etc.

As I walk my dog, I pray for my neighborhood and county. I ask the Holy Spirit to invade every home, to protect us from evil, to protect the power grids, water, and food supplies. When severe weather is predicted, I ask for protection from damaging winds, tornadoes, and earthquakes.

Even the Church needs our prayers. Many leaders in the body of Christ have watered down the gospel. Instead of unity, we see church splits. Instead of repentance, we see celebration of sin.

The Apostle Paul warns us in 1 Timothy 4:1 about deception creeping into the church. Summarize his warning below.

Deception is one of the main weapons Satan uses against us. Often a combination of some truth coupled with a lie, deception makes it difficult to discern if we do not have a solid grasp of what God has actually said in His Word. Remember how Eve was deceived when the enemy twisted God's words and added his own? In Genesis 2:16–17, God gave Adam and Eve permission to eat of every tree in the garden except the tree of the knowledge of good and evil. But how did Satan change God's command in Genesis 3:1? Write the question he asks Eve below.

Satan misquoted God and deceived Eve. Words matter when it comes to discerning God's truth and avoiding deception. In Hebrews 13:9 (NIV) we are warned: *Do not be carried away by all kinds of strange teachings*. The Lord knew that His truth would be corrupted in some church bodies and warned us ahead of time.

So how do we pray effectively?

Ephesians 1:22–23 defines the Church as His body—you, me, and all followers of Jesus. In Ephesians 5:25 we read that Christ loved the Church and gave His life for her. Summarize the reasons why in verses 26–27.

Christ died for our trespasses so that He could cleanse and sanctify the Church, to present her as a spotless bride.

On the night He was betrayed, what did Jesus pray in John 17:16–17? Summarize below.

The Church is sanctified by the Word of God—the truth. That is why it is important to meditate on Scripture so that it is woven into the fabric of our being. Righteous actions become second nature when God's truth inhabits our hearts, but infusing this truth into our souls is a lifelong process.

In Matthew 21:12, what did Jesus do to cleanse the temple in Jerusalem?

Jesus rid the temple of those who had turned it into a marketplace, selling doves for sacrifices. What did He say in verse 13? Write the verse below.

Just as Jesus cleansed the temple from corruption, we are to keep our bodies and spirits cleansed as well. Write 1 Corinthians 6:19–20 below.

Ask the Lord if there is any mixture (double mindedness) in your life. Is there anything that needs to be cleansed? Be diligent to keep a clean conscience so that you are a sweet aroma to God and those around you (see 2 Corinthians 2:15).

In John 17:22, Jesus prays that we, the body of believers, will be one with Christ and with the Father, just as they are one. Then in 1 Corinthians 12:12–26 the Apostle Paul describes both unity and diversity in the Church. Summarize the point he was making below.

Everyone in the Church is important, and each of us has unique gifts. We need to honor the diversity. What does verse 25 instruct us to do? Write the verse below.

Again, we see the theme of unity in the Church and of treating each other with love and care.

Here are some suggestions for prayers and declarations for the nation, community, and Church.

- *Lord, forgive our nation for turning away from You and embracing sin.*
- *Raise up godly men and women in positions of leadership in our churches, communities, states, and nation to replace those who walk in darkness. Give them wisdom to do Your will.*
- *Cleanse our nation of unrighteous laws.*
- *Cleanse the Church of false doctrines, and let unity and holiness reign in the Church.*

RIGHTEOUS ACTIONS
become second
nature when
GOD'S TRUTH
INHABITS OUR HEARTS,
but infusing
this truth into
OUR SOULS
is a lifelong process.

WEEK FIVE

DAY 1: Spheres of Authority

Who is the architect of your life? Whose blueprint do you want to follow?

One reason I did not want to commit my life to Christ during my wandering years sounded like this: *I don't want someone else telling me what to do.* Does that sound familiar to you? Have you ever felt that way?

Many of us grew up with these wrong ideas of who God is: He's a hard taskmaster; He's waiting to pounce on us when we make a mistake. Add to that our fallen human nature and it's a deadly concoction: deception plus rebellion.

Through costly mistakes, I have learned over decades that ceding control of my life to the One who created the universe, loves me unconditionally, created me in His image, and wants the best for me was the wisest decision I could have made that day. Who's the boss now? He is.

Today we will begin a discussion on authority. If that word makes you cringe, hold on. I hope to show that it's to your advantage to understand and embrace it. When we understand Christ's authority and our relationship to it, we will have confidence that when we pray in His name, He will back up our prayers with the power of the Holy Spirit. We will explore Christ's authority over the next two lessons, and finish on Day 3 with the believers' authority.

We do not need to know every detail of what God directs us to do in order to obey. In fact, we may not understand many things in our lifetime. One thing we can know: God designed you and me with specific purposes and destinies that will bring the maximum fulfillment in our lives and will glorify Him. But we must acknowledge His authority over us…every day and in everything. It's a tall order. Only with God's help can we possibly accomplish this. Our dependence on Him may feel like weakness, but it is our greatest strength.

Read Judges 6:11–15. For seven years the Midianites came against Israel and stole their harvest. God then sent the angel of the Lord to call Gideon into a God-given assignment. In verse 15, what was Gideon's reaction when he was called a mighty man of valor?

____

____

Gideon essentially labeled himself the least of the least. Despite his feelings of weakness, when he said yes to God's assignment, God gave him the courage to step out in faith. God used Gideon and only 300 men to defeat the over 100,000 Midianites ranged against them!

The next time you feel inadequate for a task, cast your cares on the Lord and put all your confidence in His power and strength, not yours. Read Romans 8:37 and write the verse below.

____

____

____

When we submit to God's authority, He delegates His authority to us as needed. That is the only way we can declare, "I am more than a conqueror through Christ Jesus." Do I feel like a conqueror when going through stressful times? Usually not. God often challenges me to do things that are a stretch for me—things that make me uncomfortable and are beyond my natural abilities. I am forced to take a risk, and when He accomplishes what only He can do through me, He gets the glory, and my faith and confidence in Him grow.

I am reminded of what 2 Corinthians 12:9 says: His strength is made perfect in my weakness. We have His promise that no matter what we are facing, He will never leave us or forsake us (see Hebrews 13:5).

The importance of understanding authority cannot be overstated. It is a key to our protection and living the full life God intended for us. We need to grasp God's authority fully in order to employ it effectively in prayer.

How do we differentiate between power and authority? Power refers to the strength to do something, whereas authority is the right to use power, to govern, or to control. God is omnipotent, or all powerful, as is Christ. However, Satan's power is limited. The Godhead's power did not change when Adam rebelled, nor did Satan's power.

To pray effectively and thwart the plans of the enemy, we need to be certain of Christ's victory over the devil. Read Colossians 2:15 and summarize below.

____

____

____

This verse assures us that Jesus triumphed over the agents (principalities and powers) of darkness on the cross. This is confirmed in Colossians 1:13. I love how the Amplified translation words this victory:

> *For He has rescued us and has drawn us to Himself from the dominion of darkness, and has transferred us to the kingdom of His beloved Son.*

It is reassuring to know that we are no longer under the *dominion*, or control, of Satan. Nevertheless, he still maintains his power. If Satan had lost his power, we would not need to be concerned with spiritual battles. He could not affect us. Obviously, he still does.

Satan still has power to inflict evil. If he tries to elbow his way into our life, we need to handcuff him as quickly as we can.

There are only two spiritual kingdoms: the Kingdom of God and the kingdom of darkness. We are either serving one or the other. As believers, we are no longer under the control of the kingdom of darkness because we have put our trust in Christ and His sacrifice for us on the cross.

If we are no longer under the dominion of Satan's kingdom, why does all the evil still come against us? Read Ephesians 2:1–3. What is Satan called in verse 2?

____

____

____

We remember that Satan is looking for whom he may devour. Although we are no longer under the dominion of darkness, he still has influence over the "sons of disobedience"—those who do not claim Jesus as Lord and who are easily affected by the prince of the power of the air. The source of evil is all around us.

I was never taught how to combat the fiery darts of the enemy, how to recognize spiritual warfare, or how to pray against it. I did not know I had any authority in the Kingdom of God. As a new believer, I felt like I had been dropped behind enemy lines, and I was trying to put out fires left and right.

To combat evil we need to be equipped to slam the door on Satan's toes whenever he tries to get an illegal foothold in our lives. By understanding the authority Jesus has, we learn what authority He gave to us.

In Daniel 7:13–14, Daniel describes a prophetic night vision in which he sees the Son of Man (Jesus) come to the Ancient of Days (God). What did God give Him?

____

____

____

Isn't it amazing that approximately 600 years before Christ, God gave Daniel a preview of the Messiah, whose authority and kingdom will never end. We are so blessed to be members of that kingdom. Read John 5:22, 27, 30 and summarize the authority that God the Father gave to Jesus.

Jesus explained that His authority comes from God, and His judgment of humanity is righteous because He only does the will of the Father. What assurance do believers have as stated in verse 24?

That's a good reason for anyone to place themselves under the authority of God and Christ! This is reiterated in John 17:1–2. Summarize verse 2 below.

Jesus has authority over life and death. What does Jesus say about his authority in Revelation 1:18?

Keys symbolize authority. Jesus took the keys to death and hell away from the devil.

In Ephesians 1:20–23 the Bible says that Christ is seated at the right hand of God in heaven, far above the powers of darkness and every name that can be named. All things are under His feet. That's total authority! What else is He head over (see verses 22–23)?

First Corinthians 12:27 affirms that we are the body of Christ. Therefore, Christ has authority over us. We still have free will to disobey or rebel, but I have learned the hard way that rebellion or disobedience just creates trouble for myself. Summarize Colossians 2:9–10 below.

All that we need to live godly, fruitful lives is found in Christ, and we are complete in Him. But that doesn't mean we won't suffer. What does Jesus say in John 16:33 about suffering?

We will face adversity, but in Christ we find victory and peace. Our ultimate reward is living eternally with Him.

In Isaiah 43:1–3 (NKJV), God reassures us with these words:

> *Fear not, for I have redeemed you; I have called you by your name; you are Mine. When you pass through the waters, I will be with you; and through the rivers, they shall not overflow you. When you walk through the fire, you shall not be burned, nor shall the flame scorch you. For I am the LORD your God, The Holy One of Israel, your Savior.*

Tomorrow we will look at the authority Jesus gave to His disciples. On Day 3 we will discuss how to exercise our authority over the enemy's power to thwart his evil plans against us.

DAY 2: Jesus' and the Disciples' Authority

Persecution arose against the followers of Jesus after He ascended to heaven (see Acts 8:1-8). Saul went from house to house dragging believers to prison. However, many believers scattered everywhere preaching the gospel, healing the sick, and performing signs and wonders. How did these believers get their power and authority? That is what we will study today.

Let's look at what Jesus said to His disciples in Matthew 10:1 (AMP):

> *Jesus summoned His twelve disciples and gave them authority and power over unclean spirits, to cast them out, and to heal every kind of disease and every kind of sickness.*

Why do you think Jesus gave His power and authority to the disciples?

____

____

____

Jesus knew He would not be with His disciples much longer, and they needed to learn how to exercise His power and authority over evil. His ministry lasted only three short years on earth. But He would not be leaving them helpless and subject to the wiles of the enemy.

We learned earlier that before His crucifixion, Jesus had promised to send the Holy Spirit. He had many things to teach the disciples, but they were not able to bear them at that time. Jesus' brief ministry here on earth did not enable Him to impart to them all they needed to know to evangelize nations and set people free from disease and demonic oppression. The Holy Spirit would guide them into all truth. Remember the Holy Spirit is also called the Counselor, the Spirit of wisdom, and the Spirit of truth—all very necessary for the tasks ahead.

Jesus instructed His disciples not to leave Jerusalem after His resurrection but to wait for the promise of the Holy Spirit. The group of 120 prayed together in the Upper Room until the Day of Pentecost when the power of the Holy Spirit came upon them.

Not only would the Holy Spirit guide and direct them, but He would *empower* them. After His ascension, the disciples would be Christ's representatives on earth. Supernatural power from God would be needed to heal the sick, raise the dead, and drive out demons.

Let's look at some of the ways Jesus exercised His power and authority while on earth. Read Mark 2:3–12. Summarize what Jesus did and said regarding the paralyzed man.

Jesus forgave the man's sins, and he was healed. The scribes who heard Jesus say, "Your sins are forgiven," reasoned in their hearts, "Who can forgive sins but God alone?" Jesus made it clear that He could either declare the man's sins were forgiven (authority) or declare he was healed (power). He demonstrated both. Read Mark 1:23–27 and summarize below.

Jesus rebuked the unclean spirit in a demon-possessed man and commanded it to leave. In verse 27, what was the reaction of those in the synagogue who witnessed this deliverance, and how did they describe what Jesus did?

All who saw this demonstration of authority questioned among themselves and were amazed that Jesus commanded unclean spirits with *authority*, and the spirits obeyed Him.

In contrast to the people's reaction, look at how the unclean spirits responded to Jesus' presence (Mark 1:24 NKJV).

> *Let us alone! What have we to do with You, Jesus of Nazareth? Did You come to destroy us? I know who You are—the Holy One of God!*

Isn't it interesting that those evil spirits had *no* difficulty identifying who Jesus was and what authority He possessed?

Read Luke 7:11–14. We see Jesus demonstrate His power and authority over death. What happened in those verses?

Jesus raised the widow's son from death to life. Jesus also raised Lazarus from the dead after he had been entombed for four days (see John 11:1–44). If anyone doubted Christ's authority over death, He made it clear in reference to His own death in John 10:18. Write the verse below.

Jesus explained that He even had the power over His own death. He had the power to lay down His life and to take it up again.

Jesus also demonstrated His power and authority over nature. What did He do in Matthew 8:23–27? Summarize those verses below.

Jesus took authority over the weather and calmed the violent storm. Since He took part in creating the earth, He had power over creation (see John 1:1–3).

In Mark 8:1–9, we read of another demonstration of Jesus' power. Summarize what He did below.

Why do you think we read of so many instances of Jesus exercising power and authority? Write your thoughts below.

Jesus explains the reason in John 10:37–38. Summarize His explanation below.

People questioned Jesus' claim to be the Son of God. Jesus pointed to the signs and wonders that He did as proof that He is God's Son. If people would not believe His teachings, then at least they should believe the works that He did as a confirmation that He and the Father are one.

Some Jews decided to stone Jesus for making Himself out to be God (see John 10:31–33). This was blasphemy to them. In addition, those signs and wonders had drawn thousands of people to Jesus, causing the religious leaders to fear losing their power and influence over the people. For those reasons they would eventually orchestrate His crucifixion.

Jesus knew that in order to spread the gospel after His ascension to heaven, He would need to delegate, or authorize, not only His disciples, but other faithful followers to do the works that He did as a testimony to the truth they would share. Read Luke 9:1–6 and summarize below.

First, Jesus sent out the twelve disciples and gave them authority and power over evil spirits and to heal all kinds of disease. They were commissioned to do so in every town they entered. Read Luke 10:1–2, 9 and summarize below.

After sending out the twelve disciples, Jesus further commissioned seventy followers to do the same works that He did, saying the Kingdom of God had come to them.

What was the reaction of the seventy upon their return (verse 17, NKJV)?

They rejoiced that they were able to exercise authority over the power of demons in Jesus' name.

Read Matthew 28:16–20. These verses are known as the Great Commission. Jesus had risen from the tomb and appeared to the eleven disciples to give them their lifelong assignment. They were to go and preach the good news of salvation through repentance to everyone.

In verse 18, what does Jesus say about His authority?

____

____

____

In verses 19–20, He gives the Great Commission to go and make disciples of all nations, teaching them to "observe all things that I commanded you." Then Jesus ascended to heaven.

Read Acts 2:1–4. What happened to those who gathered to pray and wait in Jerusalem for what Jesus had promised?

____

____

____

After Christ ascended to heaven, on the Day of Pentecost, the believers were all filled with the Holy Spirit. The arrival of the Holy Spirit made such a loud sound that many who had made a pilgrimage to Jerusalem wondered what had just happened. What did Peter instruct them to do in verse 38, and what did he promise would happen?

____

____

____

Verse 41 tells us that 3,000 were baptized on that day.

What additional declaration did Peter make in verse 39? Write the verse below.

____

____

____

The gift of empowerment through the Holy Spirit is promised to *all* who receive Jesus Christ as Lord and Savior. That gift was not limited to just the disciples, but to all who were from afar and to their children.

Remember what Jesus said in John 14:12? Anyone who believes in Jesus will do what He did and even greater works. Jesus' promise applies to *whoever* believes in Him. That includes us!

To accomplish the same works as Jesus did requires having power and authority over evil. For our prayers to be effective, we need to know how to exercise that authority. Tomorrow we will see how it applies to ordinary believers like you and me.

DAY 3: The Believer's Authority

At age thirteen, I had a meeting with our pastor prior to going through confirmation. I had no clue what I was doing; confirmation was just something kids my age did in our church. I will never forget what the pastor said to me with firm conviction: "Jane, God has a plan for your life." *A plan? What did that mean?* I had no idea what he meant, and he never explained it further. God was way out there in the cosmos, or so I thought. Only after I committed my life to Christ and began experiencing a personal relationship with Him did I start to discover His plans for me. God's plans would require a lot of prayer and knowledge of how to operate using His authority.

In yesterday's lesson we talked about Jesus having all authority in heaven and on earth. Before He ascended into heaven, Jesus gave that authority to His disciples. He also said that *whoever* believes in Him would do the same works and even greater works.

We are His "whoever." You might be wondering: *What does that look like for me?*

First, we must understand that although we all have access to God through prayer, we have different levels of authority based on the assignments He gives us and our levels of spiritual maturity. Authority comes from intimacy with the Lord.

We need to operate in the sphere of authority to which we are *assigned*. Our first sphere is where we have the greatest authority: over our life, our family, and our home. We have the right to ask God for our needs, to declare His promises, and to intercede for protection over ourselves and those in our care. We do that using the authority He delegated to us.

When we pray "in Jesus' name," we are praying in the *authority* He has delegated to us. When we exercise His authority, the Holy Spirit empowers our prayers. This is how we are to represent Christ on earth and do the works that He did.

A second sphere would be the right to exercise authority and intercede in an area assigned to us. When I served as a team leader over young people on a mission trip, I had authority over my team, but not another leader's team. If you are called into ministry, you have an even broader sphere over the people you are responsible for. It is important to operate in your spheres of authority and not to overstep your boundaries.

As a medical student on call for neurology, I was awakened by my beeper in the wee hours of the morning to see a new admission to the university hospital. I hurried to the bedside where a mother stood reading Scripture over her comatose son. He had suffered severe headaches for days while doing Army maneuvers in the desert out west. No one knew those headaches were signaling that a brain aneurysm was about to rupture, sending him unconscious to our hospital. I found out later that I had been summoned by mistake, but it was no mistake in God's view.

When I stood beside the bed of that comatose young man, I had no idea this event was a foreshadowing that prayer would become a major assignment in my life. In the days that followed, I watched him being tested for brain function and awareness. He did not respond to pain, sound, or touch. His eyes were open, but he did not speak or indicate any awareness of our medical team or his mother. The prognosis was hopeless. He would live the rest of his days in a vegetative state. But God...

His mother and I believed that God could do anything, so we persisted in praying for his full recovery. It took time, but his speech returned, and he eventually walked out of that hospital!

That was God's assignment for me at that time. He delegated His authority, and the Holy Spirit empowered our prayers. Other assignments would follow.

Are you aware that God has plans and a purpose for your life? If so, describe that below. If not, we will be exploring that truth in this lesson.

____

____

____

Earlier in our study, we read Psalm 139:16, which says that God saw us in the womb and had already written out a plan for our lives. What does Jeremiah 29:11 say? Summarize the verse below.

____

____

____

God's plans are to give us a future and a hope. Those plans include not only our personal hopes and dreams, but Kingdom assignments as well. In addition to praying for yourself and your family, you may feel called to intercede for issues like poverty or prison reform, similar to my call to pray for the passage of the Heartbeat Bill.

Your assignment to pray comes with a measure of authority and responsibility. Ask the Holy Spirit what to decree, write it down (so you don't forget), and persevere in prayer. Your decrees should be in agreement with God's Word in order to exercise Christ's authority and God's will. The most powerful decrees are those that come straight from the Scriptures. They are like light sabers that penetrate and shatter the darkness.

We learned earlier that we were created for good works which God planned before we were born (Ephesians 2:10). God timed your birth to be on this earth at this time and place, and He already had written a blueprint for your life. Your birthday was no accident. It was planned regardless of the circumstances surrounding your conception and the difficulties you may have suffered since then. If abortion had been legal when I was conceived, I would probably not be here writing this Bible study. Just because we may not have been a wanted child does not mean the Lord does not have a plan for our lives. Read 1 John 5:19 and write the verse below.

Unfortunately, the enemy has plans for us as well. Satan wants to abort God's destiny for our lives. That is why we need to know our authority as believers when we pray. We need to know how to block the schemes of Satan so that we fulfill our God-given assignments and destinies. Read Luke 10:19 and write the verse below.

Jesus gave us authority and power over evil spirits (serpents and scorpions) and over all the power of the kingdom of darkness.

We need to be confident that we are not under the enemy's feet; he is under ours. Read Ephesians 2:5–6. In verse 6 where does it say we are seated in the spiritual realm?

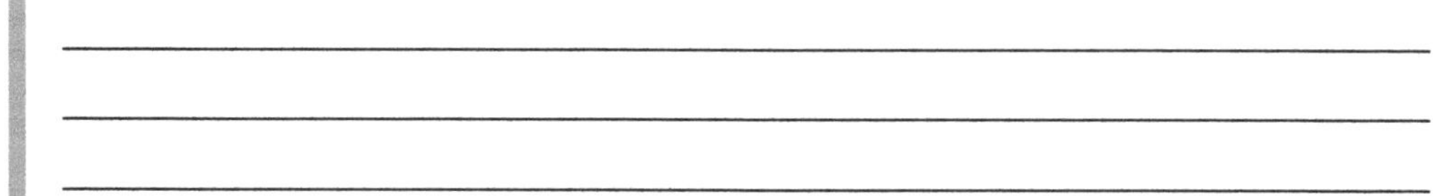

Ephesians 1:20–23 says that Christ is seated at God's right hand above every evil power. God put all things under His feet. Since we are seated with Christ, this position gives us authority over the kingdom of darkness. We need this confidence to exercise dominion over darkness.

Jesus tells us how to exercise His authority over the powers of darkness in Matthew 16:19. Write what Jesus said below.

> ____
> ____
> ____

The keys of binding and loosing (forbidding or permitting) are powerful keys of authority that Jesus gave to the Church. We are to be spiritual legislators who bind or disallow what is not allowed in heaven. We also have the authority to loose or release what already exists in heaven ("on earth as it is in heaven").

Within our spheres of authority, we have the right to bind the powers and forbid the assignments of the enemy. However, we do not have the right to bind or control another person's will. Every person has free will to obey or disobey God, to cooperate with or refuse the temptations of the enemy.

What types of things might we bind and loose? We can bind and forbid poverty and lack, sickness, injuries, and opposition—any plans of the enemy to steal, kill, and destroy. We then loose the opposites of what we bind: provision, prosperity, health, healing, and favor.

We can even affect the atmosphere around us using the keys of the Kingdom. For example, I was standing in line to buy tickets to a children's program at a local park. Three young siblings in front of me began to squabble. The line was not moving, and I was concerned that these kids' unpleasant behavior might last for quite a while. I quietly bound the powers of darkness causing strife and division and loosed peace and unity over them. In a very short amount of time, they went back to being pleasant and kind to each other for the rest of the wait.

When our children began stirring up the atmosphere in our home, I would often do the same thing; I bound what I perceived to be the spirit behind the issue and released the opposite. That did not preclude correcting behavior or issuing timeouts, but I was amazed by how releasing peace into our home actually worked. This was confirmed at my daughter's high school graduation party when one guest remarked, "Your home is so peaceful."

I am not trying to overemphasize evil, but if we are not aware that we can take dominion over the enemy's schemes, we can get blindsided. The keys to the Kingdom of God enable us to use Christ's authority over the power of the kingdom of darkness. We need to use those keys with confidence to thwart the plans of the enemy and fulfill the blueprint for our lives.

Before binding and loosing something, declare your authority and God's protection over yourself and your family by asserting Luke 10:19 and Matthew 16:19. Always make your declarations out loud since the enemy cannot read your thoughts. This puts the kingdom of darkness on notice that you are asserting your God-given authority. My declaration will sound like this:

> *I have power and authority over all the power of the enemy, and nothing shall by any means harm me and my family. Whatever I bind on earth is bound in heaven, and whatever I loose on earth is loosed in heaven. I now bind any evil spirits causing hopelessness and despair in my home (or name of family member). I release God's hope and encouragement. Let joy fill our home (or our family member), in Jesus' name.*

As parents we even have a measure of authority over evil concerning our adult children. They have free will and can choose to step out from under God's protection, but we can pray against the schemes of the enemy and add a layer of protection over and around them.

Tomorrow we will explore more tools to block the fiery darts of the devil.

DAY 4: Spiritual Warfare

My friends would probably describe me as gentle and quiet, but inside is a warrior! My competitive nature loves winning, especially at sports. Back in high school, my favorite sport was fencing—such satisfaction fending off my opponent with my sword.

Are you aware that all believers need a sword?

Ephesians 6:10–18 describes the spiritual warfare that every one of us faces on a daily basis. When we find ourselves continually at odds with someone—a family member, a coworker, or boss—we might want to consider the spiritual component of the conflict. Or perhaps we are plagued with fears, anxiety, or frequent physical ailments. If we don't ask the Lord what the source of our trouble is, we may miss the opportunity to get to the real root and deal with it spiritually, if needed.

Paul warned that we are in a battle not with other people (flesh and blood), but with evil entities (powers, principalities, rulers, and spiritual hosts) from the kingdom of darkness (Ephesians 6:12). These evil spirits can stir up strife, inflict infirmities, and oppress people—even believers.

Early in my Christian walk, I dismissed any such thing as evil spirits and spiritual battles, until I read a book that claimed a significant number of children, even in Christian homes, have had encounters with evil entities. *Ridiculous*, I thought. Having just put our children to bed, I decided to test it out. I reentered one of the bedrooms and asked, "Has anything evil ever happened to you in this room? Anything scary hiding under your bed?" Relieved to get a negative response, I walked over to the closet door. As I reached for the doorknob, I was shocked to hear one of my children say, "DON'T OPEN THAT DOOR!"

Obviously, something was frightening my child, and I needed to take care of it. But how? First, I declared we would be safe, then I stepped into the closet, faced my child, and mustered up confidence to say, "Whatever evil is in this closet, get out in Jesus' name and do not come back."

It worked! We were both thrilled, and I was now on a hunt to learn everything I could about spiritual warfare.

Paul had good reason to warn us about these battles. He faced a great deal of hardship on his missionary journeys. Thankfully, he taught us to put on the armor of God and explained each piece. After the incident above, we began praying and putting on the armor every day before the children headed off to school. Instead of using the order listed in verses 14–17, we made it easier to remember by listing the pieces from head to toe: the helmet of salvation, breastplate of righteousness, belt of truth, shoes of the gospel of peace, sword of the Spirit, and shield of faith. I still do this first thing every morning.

Why is it important to do this daily? Read verses 11 and 16 and summarize below.

____

____

____

Since the enemy is prowling around looking for whom he may devour, it stands to reason he will look for those who are unprotected. The armor quenches his fiery darts and enables us to withstand his evil schemes.

While all the pieces are important, I want to emphasize the belt of truth, the sword of the Spirit, and the shield of faith and how they are interconnected.

Truth is important as Scripture says people perish for lack of knowledge or truth (Hosea 4:6). The Holy Spirit is the Spirit of truth; therefore, we can pray for discernment when we think we are being afflicted by evil. When I suspect that evil is afoot, I will ask the Lord, "What is Your truth about this?" and sit quietly waiting for anything He might show me. Then I use the keys of the Kingdom to bind up any evil spirits and declare God's protection and blessing.

Read Matthew 4:1–11. Describe what happened to Jesus when the Spirit led Him into the wilderness.

____

____

____

Jesus was tempted by Satan to disobey God. How did Jesus counteract these temptations?

____

____

____

In verse 4 (NKJV) Jesus says: *Man shall not live by bread alone, but by every word that proceeds from the mouth of God.* The Greek for "word" in this case is *rhema*, which means Scripture that is spoken and which is specific to the situation at hand. By declaring Scripture, Jesus was using the sword of the Spirit, which is the Word of God. Hebrews 4:12 (NKJV) describes the word of God as *living and powerful, and sharper than any two-edged sword.* That is why declaring Scripture out loud with confidence is so effective against evil. What does Isaiah 55:11 say about the power of God's Word?

___

___

___

The Lord assures us that His words will accomplish what they were sent to do. Jesus succeeded in thwarting Satan with the power of God's Word. You can too.

Read 2 Samuel 22:31 and write what David said about God.

___

___

___

Our faith in God's Word acts like a shield, but we must raise up that shield every day by declaring His words of protection. I do that each morning by personalizing Job 22:28 and Psalm 91 (based on the Amplified version) and declaring them out loud. The first few verses would sound like this:

> *I shall decide and decree a thing, and it shall be established for me, and the light of God's favor will shine upon my ways. I decree Psalm 91 over (list the names): We dwell in the secret place of the Most High, and we shall remain stable and fixed under the shadow of You, Almighty God, whose power no foe can withstand.*

What does Psalm 91:4 say about our shield?

___

___

___

God's truth is His Word. By raising our shield of faith and affirming His Word over ourselves, our families, and our difficulties, we will not be afraid of the *terror of night, nor of the arrow that flies by day, nor of the pestilence that stalks in the darkness* (verse 5–6, AMP). Read Romans 10:17 and write the verse below.

___

___

___

Since faith comes by *hearing* the Word of God, our faith and our shield increase when we hear ourselves assert His truth aloud over our circumstances.

A word of caution: Ask God if there are any holes in your armor such as unconfessed sin or fear. Deal with those when you put on your armor by confessing any sins, loosing yourself from any fear, and asking God to seal up any holes.

It only takes minutes to start your day in faith, not fear. I love what someone said about faith. Faith is not denying your troubling circumstances; it is denying your circumstances the power to control you. Filling your thoughts with the truth of God and His promises pushes out fear, doubt, and worry even if you have to repeat Scriptures a dozen times a day during tough times.

In addition to the armor of God and Psalm 91, I add another layer of protection to myself and my family by pleading the blood of Jesus over our home, our possessions, our health, and our finances. Revelation 12:11 says we overcome the enemy by the blood of the Lamb and the word of our testimony (our confession of His truth).

When we use the words, "I plead the blood," we are using a legal term. An attorney pleads his case by presenting his evidence. Satan has no legal authority to come against you, even though he will try. You can defend yourself by saying, "The blood of Jesus is against you, Satan, and all your evil assignments. You have no authority over me."

When I travel, I plead the blood of Jesus over any form of transportation I will be using. When I arrive at my hotel, I declare His blood over the building. Before I unpack, I ask forgiveness for any sins committed in my room, bind any evil spirits that had access to the room, and command them to leave. Then I plead the blood of Jesus over the door, windows, and contents of the room.

We learned in a previous lesson that anointing oil was used to consecrate priests to the Lord and to cleanse all the furnishings in the Tabernacle. The oil is not magical; it is a symbol of the presence and power of the Holy Spirit—God within us. The oil represents our faith in God, His power to sanctify us, empower us, and protect us.

When I sense our family is under oppression, I take oil and anoint the lintels over the doors of our home and plead the blood of Jesus over the entrances, declaring our home off limits to the enemy.

You can use any type of oil by praying that God would anoint and consecrate it for His purposes. When I sense a lot of warfare over my thoughts, I will even apply anointing oil to my temples saying, *"In the name of the Father, Son, and Holy Spirit, I anoint my mind. I have the mind of Christ. I bind and silence all communications from the kingdom of darkness."*

What did the Lord command the Israelites to do in Exodus 12:21–23 to protect them from the last of the ten plagues of Egypt?

____

____

____

Isn't it reassuring to know that God has given us tools to protect ourselves and our loved ones? Tomorrow we will look further into some of the ways Satan tries to deceive us.

DAY 5: Avoiding Deception

The hunched-over figure on my front porch dressed in a black pointed hat and cloak unnerved me, despite it being trick or treat night. This "witch" suddenly pressed in through the door. Just as I was about to push her out, I heard my son next to me say, "Grandma?"

What? How did my son know it was my mother? She was unrecognizable. She took off her hat and mask, delighted at having fooled me so completely. Her shoes were the tipoff for my son.

Our topic today is deception, how to recognize it, avoid it, and triumph over it.

Before Jesus sent the disciples out to minister, He gave them a warning. Read Matthew 10:16 and write the verse below.

As mentioned yesterday, we are in a spiritual battle. If we ignore it, we pay the price even with minor harassments from evil spirits. They can be subtle, so it is important to seek the Holy Spirit for wisdom and discernment.

Read Acts 16:16–18. Describe how Paul and Silas were being harassed.

Although the slave girl was speaking truth, she was harassing Paul and Silas. Some think she was mocking them. After several days of being annoyed by her announcements, Paul recognized an evil spirit was trying to harass them. He took authority and commanded it to leave.

Many times the attacks of the enemy are small and difficult to discern. We may conclude easily that it's just something we did. For example, every day for years I would experience a foreign body sensation in either one of my eyes. I never prayed about it. I just assumed a tiny speck of eye makeup had dislodged and gotten into that eye. I would rinse the eye, and the sensation would disappear. This occurred so frequently that I stopped wearing a certain eye shadow; maybe that was the cause. But it continued. So I stopped wearing mascara. No change. I was buying eye drops continuously, it seemed. Then one day my eye irritation happened six times! That got my attention. The enemy had overplayed his hand. The next time it happened, instead of rinsing my eye, I bound any evil spirits that were causing it. I commanded the irritation to go and pled the blood of Jesus over that eye. Within a minute it was gone. Read James 4:7 and write the verse below.

____

____

____

Resisting the enemy doesn't cost a dime. If we don't resist, he won't flee. But it may take persistence on our part to make him leave and stay away. The battle over my eyes continued for several weeks, but by persevering, the attacks finally decreased and then disappeared! Rarely will I experience a recurrence, but then I simply state my authority and command it to go. Read John 8:44. What are some of the words that Jesus uses to describe Satan?

____

____

____

Jesus calls Satan the father of lies. Deception is the name of his game. For over twenty years every winter, I experienced brief bouts of severe stabbing pain in my right ear, which I *assumed* was the result of a case of frostbite in college. When I finally asked a rheumatologist about it, he gave me a funny look. He'd never heard of such a side effect. It was another case of deception. Over several weeks, I took authority over any evil spirits whenever it recurred and have been pain free ever since. My mistake was to *assume* the source instead of asking God what the truth was.

What does it hurt to pray? Not every health issue or problem is a deception, but now I'm much more alert to the possibility.

Read 2 Corinthians 10:3–5 and summarize Paul's description of warfare. Pay attention to what we are to take captive.

____

____

____

Paul knew that many of the battles we fight are in our thoughts. Not everything that pops into our mind is truth. We need to hold our thoughts up to the light of God's Word.

Mark 7:21 tells us that out of the heart of human beings come evil thoughts. Whether it's by the enemy or our own hearts, we can be deceived. Knowing Scripture, placing ourselves under God's authority, and praying daily to be led by the Holy Spirit are keys to avoid deception. What does 1 Corinthians 3:18–19 say about man's wisdom?

It is humbling to recognize that our hearts may deceive us, and our logic and reason may fall short of God's truth and His best for us. Our motives may be flawed, and our opinions and reasoning may be skewed. We would be wise to ask the Holy Spirit to lead and guide us daily. One of my morning prayers is: *"Lord, fill me with Your Spirit of truth and wisdom. Show me the way I should walk and the thing I should do. Put Your desires in my heart. Not my will, but Yours."*

Our emotions can also deceive us. They are real, but they may not be telling us the truth. Fear, worry, anxiety, and discouragement are the most common. Behind every emotion is a thought, and the thought might be a deception. Negative thoughts may be playing in the background of our minds like elevator music; we may not be aware that they are triggering negative emotions.

When I began paying attention to the thoughts running through my head, I was amazed at how often they were negative and how they were affecting my emotions. The next time you experience a negative emotion, ask the Lord what thought triggered that discouragement or anxiety. Then ask what His truth is because His truth will set you free.

God's truth is your sword. When He shows you the truth, renounce the deception and declare what He showed you. Even if you cannot control your circumstances, you can control your thoughts—how you view and interpret your situation. When you see your circumstances through God's eyes, you will experience peace, not fear or anxiety.

Fear comes from Satan and is one of the most common ways he attacks us. Because money was tight when I grew up, I developed a fear of poverty and lack. Years ago, I finally dealt with that fear by asking the Lord what His truth is. Read Psalm 34:10. What are we promised?

I repented for not trusting God to supply my need. Even though I knew that Scripture in my head, I have had to meditate many times on God's promises to provide and to declare these promises whenever Satan tries to invoke that fear again.

When we pray and ask the Lord for wisdom, how do we know who is speaking to our spirits—is it the Lord, our flesh, or the enemy?

The enemy will tell us half-truths or twist Scripture, just as he did to Eve in the Garden (see Genesis 3:1). His communications are demanding, harsh, or contradictory to Scripture. Pay attention to whether those thoughts or impressions are accompanied by negative emotions like fear or anxiety, or if you feel pressured to act quickly. God leads us gently; Satan pushes us.

God's words will not violate Scripture and are accompanied by peace and love. Ask for confirmations and seek wise counsel if you are not sure you are being directed by the Lord or your flesh, especially when there is a lot at stake regarding your decision. I often pray, *"Lord, put a check in my spirit if what I am sensing is not of You. Cause any thoughts to fade away if they are from my flesh. I want Your will, not mine."*

When I first began praying and listening, I practiced discernment by testing out what I felt might be the Lord on low-risk issues like buying presents, so that if I made a mistake it would not cost me a lot of time or money. Here is good advice from Paul in 1 Thessalonians 5:21. Write the verse below.

____

____

____

The Amplified translation says it this way: *Test all things carefully [so you can recognize what is good]. Hold firmly to that which is good.* You will need practice to discern the source of thoughts and impressions when you are listening for God's guidance. We will make mistakes as none of us is perfect, but we have far more to gain by seeking the Lord and His wisdom than we do by relying on ourselves. God is honored, we are humbled, and our intimacy with the Lord goes deeper when we seek Him first and spend time listening for His response.

We are heading into the final week where we will tackle topics such as learning from mistakes, staying in faith for the long haul, and recognizing blocks and hindrances to answered prayer.

WEEK SIX

DAY 1: Having Faith for the Long Haul

Congratulations! You are headed to the finish line in this final week of our study. You have persevered, and that is the topic for our next two lessons.

Prayer is a labor of love...and endurance. If you have ever given birth to a baby or have been present when a loved one has given birth, you remember how much pushing needs to happen before the baby is born. Who would give up after an hour or two and call it quits? Would any woman pack up her things and head home, too busy or too tired to see the labor till the end? Of course not.

Yet when it comes to prayer, we can become so discouraged and start questioning whether we are being heard or whether it is God's will to answer our prayers. After months or a year or two, has He forgotten us? Is He too busy with more important things? Does He even care about our problem? While God's answer to our prayers is sometimes a "no" or "wait," we must also remember that often God's "yes" takes time.

Read Daniel 10:2–14. How long had Daniel prayed before he received an angelic visitation? What explanation did the angel give for the delay?

____

____

____

We see in this passage that despite fasting and praying, Daniel's prayers weren't answered for three weeks because of spiritual warfare.

Read Luke 2:25–38. Consider Simeon and Anna. What did God promise Simeon?

____

____

____

The Lord kept His promise to Simeon. How long had Anna prayed in the temple?

____

Anna was in her eighties and spent her entire widowed life fasting and praying night and day at the temple. That is persevering faith! She was rewarded for her perseverance by seeing Jesus, the Messiah. By God's providence, both Simeon and Anna were in the temple at the exact time that Joseph and Mary presented Jesus for dedication to the Lord. God's timing was perfect for them, and it will be perfect for you too.

Read Genesis 15:1–6. What did God promise Abram?

God's promise was fulfilled in Genesis 21:1–7. How old was Abraham when Isaac was born (verse 5)?

Abraham and Sarah had to wait 25 years to see God's promise fulfilled. Is anything too hard for God?

Have you been praying and waiting a long time for something, or have you given up on God answering your prayers? Jot your thoughts below.

I love quick answers to prayers, but I have been waiting decades for others to be answered. I figure I can't lose if I don't give up.

What does 2 Peter 3:8 say about God's view of time? Summarize the verse below.

God's perspective on time is much different than ours, but He does hear every prayer, and your needs matter to Him. In Revelation 5:8, John sees the twenty-four elders in heaven's throne room with harps and bowls. What is in those bowls?

Our prayers are a sweet fragrance to the Lord, like incense, and daily they come before God's throne. When I feel frustrated waiting for an answer to my prayers, sometimes I think about those bowls—about filling them so full that they spill over with the answer. Here's a verse that might encourage you. James 5:16 (AMP) says:

> *The heartfelt and persistent prayer of a righteous man (believer) can accomplish much [when put into action and made effective by God—it is dynamic and can have tremendous power].*

Heartfelt, persevering prayers will release tremendous *power* in God's timing. Keep praying!

Romans 12:12 (NLT) exhorts us to *rejoice in our confident hope. Be patient in trouble, and keep on praying.* Persevering in anything is more difficult nowadays than in times past. We are so accustomed to fast food, high-speed Internet, and microwave meals. Who wants to wait much anymore? Like the tortoise and the hare, slow and steady wins the race when it comes to praying with perseverance.

Have you ever watched the Olympic rifle competitions? Contestants focus on the target, rather than being distracted by the competitors next to them. What we focus on matters. We cannot let circumstances or those around us deter us from persisting in prayer if we want to see results.

According to Hebrews 12:1–2, how are we supposed to run this race of life, and who are we to focus on as we run?

____

____

____

Sometimes my feet feel like they are socked in cement when times are tough. It takes effort to throw off burdens and encumbrances, to keep praying and moving forward. Feelings can weigh us down and slow us down. To run with endurance, we need to keep our eyes on the Lord.

Read Numbers 13:30–33. Moses sent twelve men to spy out the Promised Land. Caleb came back with a good report. In verse 30, what did he say?

____

____

____

Caleb had confidence in God that the land of Canaan would be theirs. However, what was the report of the ten other men as stated in verses 31–33?

Caleb focused on God's ability to fulfill His promise, whereas the other men looked only at themselves and the inhabitants occupying the land. When we put our attention on the giants in our lives, we will feel like grasshoppers. That mistake cost the Israelites forty years of desert wanderings.

Don't focus on how hard it might be to change your circumstances, and get derailed. Don't be intimidated. Take any negative thoughts captive, rise up in faith, and be a giant killer. God is fighting for you and with you through your prayers. Read Psalm 23:2–3 and write the verses below.

If you tend toward perfectionism or a type A personality, you might find it hard to lay down your to-do list and let go of your burdens. The Lord promises us rest when we spend time quietly seeking His presence.

It may take time to learn to be quiet, silence your thoughts, and invite the Lord to speak to you. You may experience a peaceful silence, but it is not wasted time if you do not sense or hear anything in your spirit. It is an investment in your relationship with God.

When we are struggling, we can remind ourselves not to be anxious, but in all things to pray with thanksgiving (see Philippians 4:6). The Lord knows we will have times of stress and anxiety, but He is saying that in every situation we are to let Him know our needs and stay thankful. What will result from those prayers? The answer is found in Philippians 4:7.

Read Isaiah 26:3 and write the verse below.

God's peace is priceless. It comes to us through prayer and a heart of thanksgiving that trusts and focuses on Him.

When the Israelites wandered in the desert, they had visible signs of God's presence, protection, and provision in the pillars of cloud and fire and the manna and quail. Once they reached the Promised Land, all that disappeared. They would then need to remind themselves of how God protected and provided for them in the desert in order to trust Him to provide in the days and years ahead.

What has God done in your life that you can look back on and be strengthened in your faith while you wait for your prayers to be answered? Write your thoughts below.

Like the Israelites, we may easily forget God's faithfulness in the past if we do not record it. If you are discouraged, pull out your list of answered prayers and read until your hope is restored. Living in light of what He has already done is a faith builder.

According to 1 Thessalonians 5:18, what are we to do no matter our circumstances?

Giving thanks in everything does not mean we thank the Lord for evil or tragedy. God is not the author of those things. We ask Him for His grace to overcome, His comfort for our souls, and we give thanks for the blessings He has given us and will give us.

Read Matthew 7:9–11 and summarize below. Pay attention to the kind of gifts God gives us.

____

____

____

If we have been through a prolonged period of hardship, seeing God as the giver of good gifts can be difficult. We may have to dig deeper into His Word and take our eyes off ourselves and our circumstances.

When things are going sour, I try to focus on being grateful for the beauty of His creation; it is a gift to us. Every day we have breath is also a gift. The assurance of eternal life is another.

Before we end this lesson, make a list of the things you are thankful for. Keep it in your journal or your Bible so that when the going gets rough, you can pull the list out and give thanks regardless of your circumstances. Giving thanks will lift your spirit.

DAY 2: Dealing with Delays

The wisdom of a fifteen-year-old young lady on a mission trip to Brazil amazed me. Like a sage, she said: "We're either in a trying time, coming out of one, or heading into another one." I've thought about her words many times. My "Pollyanna" inner self wants to believe that if I just get through this one rough spot, I might find extended smooth sailing on the other side. That's just not how life goes, no matter how hard we try to do everything right. We must commit to the long haul if we want to fulfill God's plans for our lives.

After my first grueling six weeks of medical school, I made a commitment that I would never quit no matter how hard it got, no matter what obstacles I had to overcome. Had I not done that, I might have caved to some of the pressures that threatened to unravel me later.

Are you committed to run your race with endurance? Please write your thoughts below.

____

____

____

What advice does James give in James 1:2–4? Write the verses below.

____

____

____

How many of us "count it all joy" when we face various trials? That is a big stretch for me. But looking back on the trials that are *behind* me, I can see that the testing of my faith has produced patience and wisdom. For that I am very grateful.

What does Romans 8:28 promise us? Write the verse below.

____

____

____

Remember that malpractice suit? In desperation I reached out to the Christian Medical and Dental Association for help. Upon hearing they had no resources to offer me, I hung up the phone and sobbed. Meanwhile, the secretary who answered my call took it upon herself to advocate for me with their board of trustees. The result? The Medical Malpractice Ministry was birthed. Members involved in a lawsuit are now paired with a physician who has already experienced a malpractice suit and are given educational materials to help them navigate the legal waters.

The Lord used what was agony for me and turned it into a blessing for other physicians. I look back on that experience with the deepest gratitude. My passion for intercession and for the Word of God was also birthed in that fiery trial.

Can you recall a time that really tested your faith and see in hindsight that God used it for good? Describe your experience below.

Why do we need to persevere in prayer? Why doesn't God just answer every prayer immediately? Several reasons come to mind. When we pray, the power of the Holy Spirit within us is being released. At times we must persevere until enough power is released to accomplish the task. Our faith and obedience, not works or striving, bring a cumulative release of God's power.

Read 1 Kings 18:42–45. How many times did Elijah have to pray before the rain came to end the three years of drought?

God's will was for the drought to end, but Elijah had to pray seven times for the rain to be released. I can almost hear you saying, "But I've prayed a thousand times, and nothing has happened." None of us enjoy waiting, but waiting matures us. Read Hebrews 11:1 and write the verse below.

Always expecting immediate answers to prayer does not require much faith. Waiting patiently on God's timing and trusting in His goodness deepens our faith and our relationship with the Lord. It demonstrates to Him that He can trust us with even more.

Another reason for delay may be our own disobedience. Has God told us to do something as part of the solution, but we forgot or failed to obey? Or perhaps He is working in the lives of others who have not yet come into alignment with the needed answer. For example, if you are applying for a job and did well in your interview, the Lord may need time to align the human resources person or his boss to come into agreement with God's will for you.

While we wait, we must guard against impatience, frustration, and even anger lest we treat God too casually, seeing Him as existing only to meet our wishes. We may even be tempted to treat prayer like a magic formula that should work on demand.

We must continually view God with reverence and awe, and not become self or problem focused. We will not always understand delays or answers to our prayers that were different than we expected. Although we cannot control the events around us, we can choose how we react to them. We may never know why God said no to something we thought would be wonderful. We must trust in His goodness and wisdom.

Our daughter longed to become a social worker ever since volunteering at a nursing home her freshman year of high school. That experience ignited a passion to work with the elderly, and she took every summer job and chance to volunteer during her high school years at one of the retirement facilities in our area.

Her plan to major in social work was crushed in her junior year of college when she was denied acceptance into the program. She switched majors, graduated, and eventually landed a job as an activities coordinator in a nearby nursing home/retirement village.

Four years later she felt led to research social work jobs online. The Lord opened the door to her dream job. She has been a social worker for almost five years now. Her prayers and perseverance paid off. What seemed impossible became reality for her.

Read Mark 11:22–24. Summarize the verses below. Can you find the five things we are to do when we meet an obstacle or hindrance?

____

____

____

In contrast, I did *not* know the Lord's will regarding the outcome of my lawsuit. Although I prayed that it would be dropped, after several months I got to the point of *also* praying "not my will, but Thy will." That addition to my prayer resulted from reading Hebrews 12:6–11.

Briefly summarize those verses below.

God disciplines those He loves. He may use difficult circumstances to teach us something. When we leave the results up to Him, God can turn our worst nightmares into blessings.

When troubling times arrive on my doorstep, I am often reminded of Luke 3:2 (NIV): The word of God came to John son of Zechariah in the wilderness. No matter how dark your circumstances seem, God has a way to speak to you in your wilderness times. What are we told to do in Psalm 46:10?

Sometimes the hardest thing to do is to be still, to keep seeking God, and to wait upon Him to speak into our situation. The Lord makes a promise to those who wait upon Him in Isaiah 40:29–31. Summarize those promises below.

Persevering in difficult times can be depleting. I often pray for more strength and more of His grace to endure. Even the prophet Elijah came to a point of giving up. Read 1 Kings 19:1–18. Queen Jezebel had threatened to kill him, so he ran for his life. How did the Lord encourage him?

Some of us may have experienced such a low point in the past that we despaired of life itself just like Elijah. However, God never gives up on us. We must not give up on Him. Like Elijah, if we persevere and trust in God's goodness, He will reveal new assignments to further His kingdom work on earth that will also bless us. The enemy is the one who pushes us to the point of desperation, making us feel hopeless and alone, hoping that we will quit.

Read the account of Joseph found in Genesis 37:1–28. Briefly summarize what happened to this seventeen-year-old.

Joseph was betrayed by his jealous brothers and sold as a slave. He became a servant in Potiphar's household in Egypt. Despite being a slave, Genesis 39:2–3 tells us something very interesting. Summarize those two verses below.

Despite his excellent service to Potiphar, he was betrayed a second time by Potiphar's wife and was thrown into prison on false charges. What did the Lord do for Joseph in prison as recounted in verses 21–23?

In all those trials as a slave and a prisoner for thirteen years, Joseph remained obedient to the Lord, and the Lord gave him favor and prospered him. He eventually became the second in command to Pharaoh.

How did Joseph summarize his fiery ordeal to his brothers when they were finally reconciled to each other? Summarize Genesis 50:20 below.

Read Psalm 105:16–21 and write verse 17 below.

From Joseph's perspective, his brothers sold him into slavery. But from God's perspective, He *sent* Joseph to Egypt to preserve his family during a famine.

We may be going through a situation that appears to have no solution, no light at the end of the tunnel. We may have prayed for years, even decades, but be assured every single one of our prayers has been heard.

How does the writer of Hebrews 10:35–36 encourage us? Write the verses below.

Our task in trying times is to stay humble, not grumble, and be obedient to the Lord. Faith plus endurance releases God's promises and rewards.

What does Paul exhort us to do in 1 Corinthians 16:13–14?

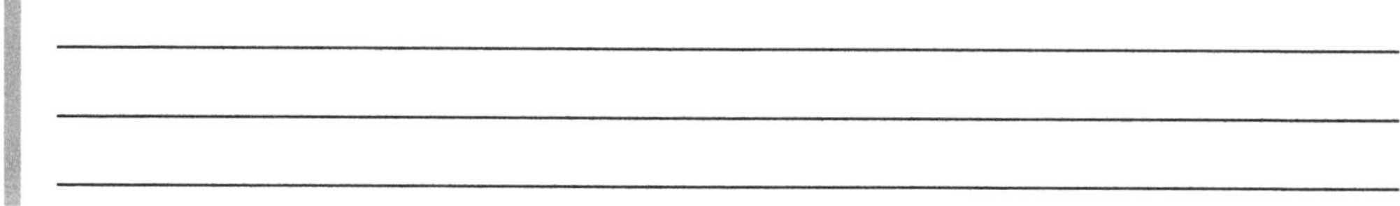

Living in dry seasons or dark nights of the soul can tax us to the limits. Do not be afraid to reach out for prayer from others, to seek counseling if needed, and to surround yourself with supportive people, not naysayers. Remind yourself daily that the Lord is with you as He was with Joseph.

As a final assurance read Psalm 34:15 and record it below.

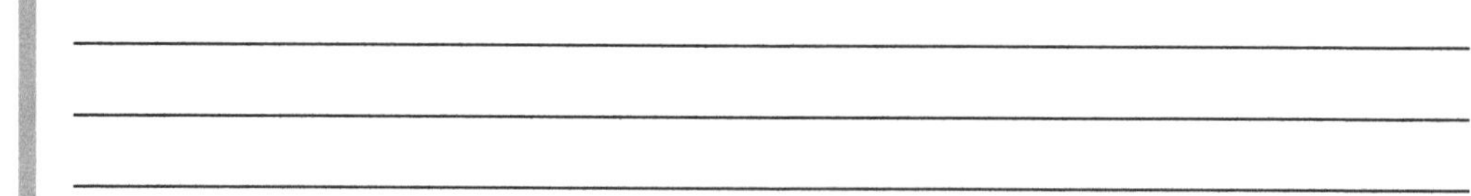

The Lord's eyes are always upon you. His ears are always tuned to your prayers. Be encouraged; stand in faith and let nothing move you.

Tomorrow we will get a peek into mistakes we might make and how to avoid them.

DAY 3: Learning from Mistakes

Many times when we pray, the biggest cause for making mistakes is located between our right and left ears—the center of our human logic and reasoning.

Let's review Romans 8:5 (AMP). The Amplified translation of this verse adds more clarity:

> *For those who are living according to the flesh set their minds on the things of the flesh [which gratify the body], but those who are living according to the Spirit, [set their minds on] the things of the Spirit [His will and purpose].*

My childhood was filled with insecurity, so as an adult I wanted as much control over my life as possible. I didn't trust God; I hardly knew Him, even after years of being a Christian. What did it mean to be controlled by the desires of the Holy Spirit?

Logic and reasoning determined everything I did. I prayed my list, ended my prayer, and then went about solving all my problems without any direct input from God. However, when I read Romans 8:6 in the Amplified translation a profound change occurred in the way I prayed.

> *Now the mind of the flesh is death [both now and forever—because it pursues sin]; but the mind of the Spirit is life and peace [the spiritual well-being that comes from walking with God—both now and forever].*

To be clear, using logic and reasoning is not wrong. Don't check your brain at the door when you pray. After all, God uses our minds and common sense. It's whether we submit our reasoning to the Holy Spirit that makes the difference. Are we choosing to operate in the flesh or by His Spirit?

Our human reasoning is no match for God's unlimited wisdom. He sees things we cannot see. He knows the future. Remember that Proverbs 3:5–6 cautions us not to rely or lean on our own understanding, but to trust the Lord in *all* our ways. When we do that, He directs our paths.

Instead of operating in the flesh with its limitations, why not rely on the Holy Spirit, asking Him to put His desires in your heart? Ask Him to quiet your flesh and direct your thoughts. Jeremiah 29:11 (AMP) says, *I know the plans and thoughts that I have for you.* His plans for us are to give us peace, a future, and a hope. That sounds like a good deal!

Read Joshua 6:1–5. Summarize the strategy God gave Joshua for conquering Jericho, a city with very high, thick walls.

____

____

____

According to human logic and reasoning, does that plan make any sense? Three walls were protecting Jericho: the retaining wall was 12 to 15 feet high; the outer city wall (on top of the retaining wall) was 20 to 26 feet tall, and lastly an inner-city wall was 46 feet above ground level.

Some of the things the Lord directs us to do might not make any sense, but a blessing awaits when we obey. If you question whether something is from God, seek wise counsel and be sure it does not violate Scripture.

Are we open to whatever the Lord directs us to do? That's a challenge! Read Isaiah 55:8–9 and write verse 8 below.

____

____

____

Why limit God? Why not go for the best answers to our prayers by being open to whatever God wants to do? Human logic that is not submitted to the Holy Spirit may limit how the Lord can direct us. Here's a simple prayer: *"Holy Spirit, take control of my thoughts, and put Your desires in my heart."*

Along the same lines, another mistake we can make is to hold strong opinions about what we are praying. I prayed with someone who had a troubled relationship and was struggling with whether to go visit. The Lord gave several confirmations that it would be unwise to do so. Unbeknownst to me, this person had a strong opinion about going, and therefore ignored the Lord's wisdom. The visit did not go well.

A similar mistake would be to put certain limits or boundaries on the Lord. Be careful if you find yourself saying, "I will never...." Some of my "I will never" statements turned out to be exactly what the Lord wanted for me, and they turned out to be blessings. How many times did I say to myself, *I will never get a dog!* as I watched neighbors walk their dogs in the rain and snow—until the Lord impressed on me to buy a Maltese.

As I was driving home with our new pet, I received a call from our daughter. Through sobs she shared the heartbreaking news that she had not been accepted into the major she dreamed of studying at college. She was devastated.

"I'll call you back. I'm almost home and we can talk about it then."

Back home, I returned her call via Skype and let her pour out her heart before lifting up the ball of white fluff sitting in my lap.

"Are you serious?" she cried. "Is he *ours*?"

My daughter is a serious animal lover. Unbeknownst to me, the Lord orchestrated the timing of my purchase to coincide with one of my daughter's worst days. My "never" helped heal her pain that day.

Oh, and the name the Lord gave our dog—BJ—stands for blessings and joy.

Jesus modeled how we are to live as Christians. He never said no to His Father. We miss God's best when we say no to Him. The same may be true for some of our "I'll nevers." Don't let them rob you of His blessings.

Presuming on God's timing instead of waiting can also get us in trouble. Read 1 Samuel 13:7-14. What happened when Saul failed to wait for Samuel to make the sacrifice? Summarize verse 13 below.

____

____

____

Saul's kingdom would no longer endure because he preempted Samuel. His presumption cost him his reign over Israel.

If you are embarking on a new path that God has led you to, beware the naysayers. They may talk you out of God's best plan for you. As I was applying to medical school, I met with some opposition. One resident (doctor-in-training) told me point blank that he didn't believe women should be doctors. A family member and some friends also tried to discourage me. Fortunately, the Lord had confirmed I was on the right track, so I chose to ignore them. Read Job 1:1–22 and briefly summarize below.

____

____

____

Job suffered horrific losses of his family and possessions, yet despite these tragedies, how did Job react? Write verse 22 below.

____

____

____

Read Job 2:4–8. What happened next to Job?

____

____

____

When Satan inflicted painful boils on Job, his wife told him to curse God and die. She comes across as the ultimate naysayer. Fortunately, Job ignored her command. Read Job 15:5–6 and 22:4–5. Summarize what Job's friend, Eliphaz, said to him.

Who needs enemies with a friend like Eliphaz? Job's other two friends also claimed that Job's sinfulness was the reason for his suffering. Sometimes when we are enduring troubling times, even those closest to us will not be supportive. That gives us even more reason to get alone with the Lord, seek Him diligently, and not allow critical voices to derail us.

Another potential source of error when we pray is to limit God by making decisions based solely on money and not on His wisdom. Read Proverbs 8:11 and write the verse below.

In the early years of my medical practice, I felt an unexplainable urge to save, save, save. It made no sense. As a two-career couple, we were certain our future earnings would be substantial. As mentioned earlier, we began plans to build our dream house. Week after week when returning from talking to builders, I would have a check in my spirit. I couldn't understand why. Our mistake—we never prayed about whether it was God's plan for us to upgrade our home. We just *assumed* we would have the finances and plowed ahead.

Only God knew that our income would be drastically reduced and that my career would be short-lived. In contrast, when I became a stay-at-home mom on a limited budget, I had to learn to obey God when I didn't know where the money would come from and trust Him to provide. Read Haggai 2:8 and write the verse below.

God has unlimited wealth that He can deliver to us at any time. God taught us to trust Him for finances. When He directed me to sign up for an out-of-state conference, I had no idea how it would be paid for. After I made the plane and hotel reservations, a friend (who did not know about my need) sent a check in the mail that covered the costs.

Just recently I prayed for a cashier that I befriended at our local grocery store. She mentioned a financial need, so I immediately prayed out loud, "Lord, multiply her finances." As I walked away, serious misgivings arose as I reasoned to myself: *How is God going to do that? Her husband already received his bonus. No raises are in sight.* I could not see any way God could bless her financially. *Maybe I shouldn't have prayed that prayer,* I thought.

The following week I was stunned to hear the results of that prayer. Within a few days, someone going through her checkout area simply handed her $60. That same day another shopper handed her $20! I'm so glad I didn't let my logic and reasoning stop me from praying for her that day. It was a good reminder to me not to limit God, as nothing is impossible with Him.

Remember, God is not expecting us to be perfect. He knows we will make mistakes. It's important to learn from them, dust ourselves off, and keep seeking Him.

Tomorrow we will look at blocks and hindrances to answered prayers.

DAY 4: Blocks and Hindrances to Prayer

A friend stopped by my apartment to visit and mentioned her desire to be married. She was taken aback by my question: "Have you prayed about it?" I was taken aback by her response: "No, God knows that's what I want." Read James 4:2. What reason does James give for why we do not have what we want?

____

____

____

True, God knew what my friend wanted, but she did not know what He wanted. He wanted her to ask. When I explained that might be the reason she had not received the desire of her heart, she took it seriously. Within weeks of praying, she met her future husband. I wish all my prayers were answered that quickly!

Are you struggling with unmet needs? Have you remembered to ask the Lord to supply those needs? Or might something be blocking the answer to your prayers? Today we will be talking about possible blocks and hindrances to our prayers.

James 4:3 (AMP) warns that if we ask and fail to receive, it could be because *you ask with wrong motives [out of selfishness or with an unrighteous agenda]*. Read Psalm 19:12 and write the verse below.

____

____

____

At times we may be deceived by our own hearts. If our prayer is not being answered, perhaps we need to ask the Lord to uncover our motives.

In Matthew 20:20–28, the mother of James and John asks a favor of Jesus. What was the favor, and what do you think her motive was?

____

____

____

Asking for prestigious positions in Jesus' kingdom was ambitious and self-serving. How did Jesus respond to her request?

Summarize verses 22–28 below.

Jesus addressed the mother's selfish motive by pointing out the proper means by which to be honored in His kingdom. He defined kingdom leadership by describing His own purpose. He came to serve, not to be served. Read Psalm 66:18 and write the verse below.

Sin separates us from God. Unconfessed sin can be another hindrance to seeing our prayers answered. Read Romans 7:19–25. Paul talks about his inner battle. Summarize his thoughts below.

Paul's transparency is reassuring. His mind and heart desire to do good; his flesh causes him to sin. We are all subject to the failings of our fallen nature, but God has provided a remedy. We can instantly repent and be assured that God does not condemn us (see Romans 8:1).

Even after we ask God's forgiveness, it is easy to keep beating ourselves up with guilt and shame, especially when we fail to forgive ourselves. The enemy may also heap on feelings of unworthiness. But Paul reassures us that there is no condemnation for those who are in Christ. Read Psalm 24:3–5 and summarize below.

The Lord asks us to come to Him with a clean heart. Our hearts are cleansed and purified through repentance and forgiveness. God is not looking for us to be perfect.

Read Matthew 6:14–15. Not only do we need to ask for our own forgiveness, but we are required to forgive those who have sinned against us. Ask the Lord whether unforgiveness might be blocking the answer to your prayers.

Have you been seeking God for wisdom? We know according to James 1:5 that if we lack wisdom, we should ask the Lord for it. James cautions us in verses 6–8. Summarize those verses below.

____

____

____

If we truly desire His wisdom, we must not be double-minded, wavering back and forth doubting He will respond. If you have asked for His wisdom, check to see if you are negating your prayers with doubt.

Proverbs 5:1 (AMP) says: *Be attentive to my wisdom [godly wisdom learned by costly experience], incline your ear to my understanding.*

Perhaps God's answer to your prayers for wisdom has actually come through costly experience, but you may not have recognized it as His answer. Read Proverbs 18:21 and write the verse below.

____

____

____

The words that we speak release power. Our prayers might be hindered because of what we have said about our situation. Many times we are not aware that we are negating our own prayers by the words we speak. What does James say about the tongue in James 3:8–9?

____

____

____

Are we praying for a better relationship with a family member, friend, or coworker but bad mouthing them when we are apart?

Read Ephesians 4:29 and 5:4. Paul warns us to avoid certain types of speaking. Summarize those below.

Years ago on a trip out of the country, I experienced first hand how powerful our words can be. It was our last day in Romania and our last chance to get the adoption paperwork approved by the court. When the four of us walked out to get in the car, we were stunned to see a flat tire. One person's first reaction was to say something negative about our seemingly hopeless situation. However, by the grace of God, faith rose up within me. What was impossible for us was possible for God, and I said, "Now is when we will see the hand of God move." Indeed, to our surprise and delight, we were able to secure the documents that day. Read Proverbs 10:11. What does it say about the mouth of the righteous?

Proverbs 12:14 (NIV) says, *From the fruit of their lips people are filled with good things.* Our prayers may be hindered when we speak contrary to Scripture or to what the Lord has already shown us to be His will.

Words may be likened to seeds that we sow. Are we sowing for a good harvest or complaining and sowing for a bad harvest? Is the fruit of our mouth pleasing and in agreement with God's Word, or are we inviting the enemy to steal the harvest by negating what God has said?

In a previous lesson we discussed how God's timing is different than ours. Sometimes we quit too soon because we think we've made too many mistakes, and why would God ever answer our prayer after all our blunders? Read Proverbs 24:16. What does it say about a righteous person?

We are righteous through the blood of Jesus Christ. When we fail (and we will), we need to get up and shake off that failure, not wallow in it. The key is not to quit. Remember—the delay may be a test of our faith to prepare us for what lies ahead. Or we may be waiting on others to align with God's answer.

The enemy of our souls may also be the reason why our prayers are not being answered right away. Remember, Daniel fasted and prayed for twenty-one days before breakthrough came (see Daniel 10:4–13). It wasn't that his prayers were not heard. A powerful spirit of darkness was delaying the answer.

I pray every time I sit down to write. In the last week of writing this manuscript, I began experiencing warfare over my computer. I knew the enemy would love to hinder the completion of this Bible study. I had to resort to prayers such as: *"I plead the blood of Jesus over my laptop: the hardware, software, and Internet connections. I bind all assignments from the kingdom of darkness. I take authority over any blocking or hindering spirits and forbid them from affecting my computer."* Be firm and repeat if necessary. It only takes seconds to take authority over the enemy's schemes. Resist the devil, and he will flee!

If you suspect God's answer may be blocked by spiritual warfare and you are experiencing resistance, do not give up. Find some prayer partners to agree with you. Prayers of agreement are powerful.

Lastly, as you continue to wait on His answers, always keep the Lord your main focus rather than your unmet need or troubling circumstances.

We will finish our study tomorrow with a summary of dos and don'ts.

DAY 5: Dos and Don'ts

You made it!

It's almost time to say goodbye. What parent has not stood at the door as a family member leaves and said, "Now remember...don't forget to..." as their loved one heads off somewhere?

Today we will go through some dos and don'ts of praying—things we don't want to forget. I created a partial checklist at the end of this lesson that you can add on to as you head out to practice what you have learned these past six weeks. Above all, don't grow weary! Read Galatians 6:9 and summarize below.

____

____

____

Satan wants to wear us out so that we give up or retreat. The Lord wants to raise up an army of prayer warriors that will persevere until they receive what they prayed for. When you feel worn down, remember Philippians 4:13: You can do all things through Christ who strengthens you.

You might feel weary, but if you will declare that verse over yourself, the Holy Spirit will empower you to keep going and keep praying. His strength is made perfect in our weakness (see 2 Corinthians 12:9). Read Ephesians 6:10 and write the verse below.

____

____

____

We may sometimes feel like we have nothing left to give, no energy to move forward. Has God *really* heard our prayers? This is when we must lean harder on Him and ask for His strength to carry us through. Don't quit! Read Psalm 91:15 and write the verse below.

____

____

____

Don't forget that you can call on the Lord night or day. He *will* answer you. He will be with you in troubled times. You will eventually come out on the other side, stronger and deeper in your relationship with Him.

Don't feel pressured to act quickly. Read Proverbs 19:2 (NIV) and write the verse below.

God does not rush us. Early in my efforts to listen to the Lord's leading, I suddenly felt an urgency to go visit an acquaintance who lived near where I was driving that day. I hurried over only to find she wasn't home. *How did I make that mistake?* I wondered.

Mistakes are inevitable; we're human. View them as opportunities to discern on a deeper level. Don't beat yourself up. I learned from my mistake that the Lord communicates with peace, not urgency or anxiety. The enemy pushes; the Lord guides peacefully.

Hone your discernment by asking the Lord what went wrong. Was the thought that popped up in your mind from the Lord, the enemy, or your flesh? Was it pushy or peaceful? Did it align with God's Word or with selfish motives?

Don't forget to lay down strong opinions. Don't rely totally on your logic and reasoning without asking for God's wisdom. Don't rely totally on a friend's advice without asking God for His truth.

It's also easy to feel pressured by what others might think of us, but listening to and obeying the Lord will protect us from unwise choices. Read Proverbs 16:18. What warning are we given in that verse?

Fear of looking foolish—pride—can cause us to miss God's best. Read 1 Peter 5:5 and summarize below.

Psalm 25:9 (NIV) says, *He guides the humble in what is right and teaches them his way.* The Lord loves to share His wisdom with those who are humble and teachable. This verse was perfectly illustrated while I was making rounds at the hospital one day.

"Would someone get me a cup of water, please?" The voice came from behind the white curtain that separated one patient's bed from another on the hospital ward where our team of medical students was making rounds. I moved toward the voice only to be stopped cold by my supervising physician.

"Let the nurse get that. You're a physician." The implication was clear; he considered it beneath our profession to tend to such a menial task.

Weeks later a couple at my church sang a worship song whose lyrics echoed that of Jesus' words in Matthew 10:42. Summarize that verse below.

____

____

____

Conviction struck me like a bucket of cold water poured over my head. The Lord was not condemning me with those lyrics, He was teaching me how to be more like Jesus. Sitting in that pew, I determined never to refuse the request of a patient that was within my means to provide. Don't let your reputation or pride keep you from serving the Lord in whatever He directs you to do.

Similarly, don't let guilt or shame determine your choices. Get alone with the Lord and ask what His truth is about your situation. Read Proverbs 2:6 and write the verse below.

____

____

____

When we pray, "Thy kingdom come, Thy will be done," what if the Lord asks us to do something out of our comfort zone? Read Hebrews 10:38 and write the verse below.

____

____

____

The Amplified translation reads: *...if he draws back [shrinking in fear], my soul has no delight in him.* I was an expert at shrinking. Goodness, how many times had I let timidity, shyness, and fear keep me from obeying His will? That verse convicted me to pray frequently for boldness and courage to step out in faith. Don't let your fears rob you of obeying the Lord. When led to do something that is a stretch for me, I pray, "Lord, take over and do that through me." Intimidation still wins out at times, but I'm making progress.

Don't give in to fear, but also don't speak words of fear over yourself or your situation. What does 2 Timothy 1:7 say about fear?

____

____

____

When you pray, don't yield to fear of failure, or fear of poverty and lack. Bind any fears and forbid them to affect you. Then ask the Lord to fill you with a spirit of power, love, and a sound mind. Fear is one of the most common attacks from the enemy. Resist it firmly, and it will leave.

Fear can create a hole in your armor. Once I had to work in close quarters with someone who was coughing and sneezing the entire time. During those two hours, I feared catching what she had. Sure enough, the next day my throat was sore. What I feared became reality. When I asked the Lord to heal my throat, He showed me that my fear of getting sick opened the door for the enemy to give me a sore throat. I repented and asked Him to remove the soreness. Several hours later it disappeared.

Don't let distractions and busyness keep you from spending time talking and listening to God. Read Luke 10:38–42 and summarize below. Pay attention to how Jesus describes Martha.

____

____

____

Martha was not simply being a hostess; she was distracted, worried, and troubled. This was a divine appointment for her household to listen to Jesus. She was missing out on the best part of His visit while Mary was soaking up His teaching. Don't be a Martha and miss out on listening to the Lord in your prayer time.

Distractions are everywhere. Don't let a cell phone or a to-do list rob you of time every morning with the Lord. I still catch myself at times sneaking a peek at my phone if I forget to mute the notifications. It takes time to quiet the monologue of worries that runs through our brains, relax, and simply sit in His presence, giving Him our full attention for whatever He might want to share from His heart that day. You may just hear silence when you listen, but don't miss any opportunity to learn from Him.

Those are some of the don'ts. You might be wondering: *What about the dos?*

Do be accountable and connected to the body of Christ. Read Hebrews 10:24–25 and summarize the verses below.

____

____

____

Meeting regularly with other believers will help you stay on track. Find a prayer group that will help you go deeper in your relationship with the Lord.

Do make the Lord your first priority every day. He will prepare you for what lies ahead.

Do make your prayers a dialogue rather than a monologue. What did Jesus say in John 10:27?

____

____

____

We need to set aside time to listen and wait for Him to speak. Avoid reading off a list of your needs when you pray or reciting all the details (He already knows them). After entering His presence with thanksgiving and praise, bring up one issue at a time. "This is what I need wisdom for." Then ask Him to reveal His truth about your situation.

Do remember to use open-ended questions that allow the Lord free rein to say anything He wants about your concerns. Avoid yes/no questions that limit the Lord to only two choices. Read Isaiah 30:21 and write the verse below.

____

____

____

Many times the Lord's answer comes at some other time when I am not in prayer. Someone might say something to me, and it's exactly what I needed to hear. Or I might read a magazine article or book, and there's the answer. The Lord is creative in how He communicates with us.

Be willing to meditate on and marinate in His Word daily. His Word is His will, and your answer may be waiting to be discovered as you dig into the Scriptures.

Be passionate about your relationship with the Lord. In Revelation 3:15–16, an angel warns the church at Laodicea not to be lukewarm. The Lord is drawn to us when we run after him with fervor.

Do *expect* to hear from the Lord. Your expectation is a demonstration of faith. Prayer is not about a formula, but an intimate, personal relationship with our Creator. He longs to hear your voice coming to Him with child-like faith.

As you listen and receive personalized answers to your prayers, your relationship with God will grow stronger and deeper. The disciples did not just have head knowledge of Jesus' teachings; they experienced His presence and His power. He wants to have a similar relationship with you. You will then become a living testimony to His love, His goodness, and His faithfulness.

Keep Jesus in the center of your life, and watch how exciting and powerful your prayer life will be!

Here is a convenient checklist to review before you begin praying.

- Isolate yourself from noise and distractions. Silence your phone.
- Invite the presence of the Holy Spirit to refill and refresh you before you begin.
- Enter His presence with thanksgiving and praise.
- Set protective boundaries:
    - > Declare Psalm 91 over yourself and family.
    - > Declare your authority over the kingdom of darkness to block interference.
        - – Declare Luke 10:19.
        - – Declare Matthew 18:18.
    - > Assert that authority:
        - – *"I bind and silence any forms of communication from the kingdom of darkness in Jesus' name."*
        - – *"I command my flesh to be silent."*
- Give the Lord honor by first asking, "What is on Your heart, Lord?" Then listen.
- If nothing comes to mind, go ahead and ask for wisdom.
    - > *"Lord, please fill me with Your spirit of truth and wisdom. What is Your truth about (name the issue)?"* Then listen. If after a few minutes there is no answer, expect that He will answer later and thank Him: *"Lord, I thank You that You will show me what I should do in Your perfect timing."* Move on to your next question.
- Test anything that you are not sure about:
    - > Does it align with Scripture?
    - > Is it accompanied by peace?
    - > If the consequences would be significant, ask for confirmations.

- Ask for your needs to be met and be specific.
- Intercede for others and whatever issues the Lord puts on your heart.
- Thank God for His answers even before you receive them.

Here's a final challenge: If you were to stand in front of a door that represents your relationship to the Lord, would the door be open a crack, an inch, a foot, or wide open? Does God have access to every area of your life or just a few?

Jesus said, *Behold, I stand at the door and knock. If anyone hears My voice and opens the door, I will come in to him and dine with him, and he with Me* (Revelation 3:20 NKJV).

Take some time right now to ask the Lord if there are any doors to any rooms of your life that are locked and off limits to Him? Are there any doors to any areas of your life that are partially open but need to be fully open? If you hesitate to let Him in those places, ask Him for the courage and the willingness to do so. You have everything to gain and nothing to lose by doing that.

If we do not continually move toward the Lord, our relationship with Him will start to stagnate. He promises us that when we seek Him, we will find Him—when we seek with *all our hearts* (Jeremiah 29:13).

I pray that your heart's desire is to experience the love of Christ and to be a vessel wholly filled and flooded with His presence (Ephesians 3:19).

Take the plunge. Open wide the door to your heart. Partnering with God may be challenging, but the rewards are priceless and eternal.

Appendix A

SCRIPTURE DECLARATIONS

Here is a list of personalized Scriptures to meditate on and declare over yourself and your family if you are struggling with negative emotions, health, or financial issues, or if you're needing wisdom or encouragement. I pray that they will comfort and strengthen you.

WISDOM

- I will trust in You, Lord, with all my heart. I will not rely on my own understanding. I will acknowledge You in all my ways, and You will make my paths straight (Proverbs 3:5–6).
- I come to You, Lord, without any doubts that as I seek You for wisdom, You will generously supply all the wisdom I need (James 1:5).
- Fill me with a spirit of truth, wisdom, and revelation (Ephesians 1:17).
- Cause my mind to be transformed and renewed by Your word, so that I come to know what Your perfect will is for me (Romans 12:2).

WORRY

- I refuse to worry about my life, what I will eat or wear, but I will seek You first and Your kingdom and Your righteousness, and everything that I need will be given to me (Matthew 6:25, 31–33).
- I will not worry about tomorrow. I choose to trust You for today (Matthew 6:34).
- I cast all my cares on You because You care for me (1 Peter 5:7).
- I refuse to worry. I will be still and know that You are God, and that You are with me (Psalm 46:10).

ANXIETY

- I will be anxious for nothing but will present my requests to You with thanksgiving, and Your peace will guard my heart and mind in Christ Jesus (Philippians 4:6–7).
- I will not allow those things that I see to cause me anxiety. I will walk by faith and not by sight (2 Corinthians 5:7).
- You are my defense; I will not be anxious. No weapon formed against me shall prosper (Isaiah 54:17).
- I will lie down and sleep in peace because You alone make me to dwell safely (Psalm 4:8).

FEAR

- I will not fear because You have not given me a spirit of fear, but of power, love, and a sound mind (2 Timothy 1:7).
- Fill me with Your perfect love that casts out all fear (1 John 4:18).
- I will not fear for You are with me. You will strengthen me and help me. You will hold me up with Your righteous right hand (Isaiah 41:10).
- I will be strong and of good courage. I will not fear because You are with me wherever I go (Joshua 1:9).

PEACE

- You will keep me in perfect peace as I keep my mind focused on You (Isaiah 26:3).
- Lord, lift up Your countenance upon me and give me peace (Numbers 6:26).
- You are the Lord of peace. Grant me peace at all times and in every way (2 Thessalonians 3:16).
- You are the God of hope. Fill me with all joy and peace in believing so that by the power of the Holy Spirit, I may abound in hope (Romans 15:13).

HEALTH

- I am prospering and enjoying good health, just as my soul prospers (3 John 2).
- I will not let Your words out of my sight. I will keep them in my heart. They are life to those who find them and health to my whole body. (Proverbs 4:21–22).
- My body is a temple of the Holy Spirit. Sickness has no authority over me (1 Corinthians 6:19).
- You sent forth Your word to heal me and deliver me from destruction (Psalm 107:20).

FINANCES

- I choose to be a cheerful giver and to sow generously. Bless me abundantly so that I have all that I need at all times to perform the good works You have for me to do (2 Corinthians 9:6–8).
- I will not trust in riches. I will be generous and have an abundance (Proverbs 11:25, 28).
- Keep my heart from the love of money. Help me be content with what I have (Hebrews 13:5).
- Every good and perfect gift comes from You, Father. May I always be thankful for Your blessings (James 1:17).

ENCOURAGEMENT

- God is working out everything in agreement with the counsel and design of His will for me (Ephesians 1:11).
- God can do all things and no thought or purpose of His can be thwarted (Job 42:2).
- Greater is He that is within me than he that is in the world (1 John 4:4).
- The enemy may attack one way, but he must flee seven ways (Deuteronomy 28:7).

Appendix B

RECOMMENDED READING

The following books are recommended by the author for further study.

Freed, Sandie. *Understanding Your Dreams*. Grand Rapids: Chosen, 2017.

Glenchur, Jane. *Seven Secrets to Power Praying: How to Access God's Wisdom and Miracles Every Day*. Grand Rapids: Chosen, 2014.

Sheets, Dutch. *Authority in Prayer*. Minneapolis: Bethany, 2007.

ACKNOWLEDGMENTS

I offer abundant gratitude to the many friends who prayed with me and for me as I wrote this study:

Carol Atkins—who faithfully and diligently read every word and offered her cogent comments. She not only made suggestions but encouraged me every step of the way.

My book club ladies—who faithfully prayed this study into being: Ginny Feeney, Cleo Jones, Marie Nicholson, Jan Ottenjohn, Lesley Price, and Diane Stevens.

Marilyn Eldridge--for her many powerful prayers and loyal friendship.

My ministry friends—for their love, support, and spiritual covering. Thank you, Darenda Keil, SueLee Jin, and Laura Harris.

My praying friends—who I can count on to pray as soon as they read my text requests: Jane Johantges, Jennifer Odom, and Laurie Gibson.

Julie Campbell—my editor at Warner Press, who invited me to write this study and was so encouraging and easy to work with.